WORLD
BOOK

AMERICA'S PRESIDENTS

S PRESIDENTS

THE PRESIDENT'S WORLD

World Book, Inc.

www.worldbook.com

Staff

Executive Committee

President
Jim O'Rourke

Vice President and Editor in Chief
Paul A. Kobasa

Vice President, Finance
Donald D. Keller

Vice President, Marketing
Jean Lin

Vice President, International Sales
Maksim Rutenberg

Director, Human Resources
Bev Ecker

Editorial

Director, Digital & Print Content Development
Emily Kline

Editor, Digital & Print Content Development
Kendra Muntz

Senior Editor, Regions
Ken Shenkman

Manager, Indexing Services
David Pofelski

Manager, Contracts & Compliance (Rights & Permissions)
Loranne K. Shields

Administrative Assistant
Ethel Matthews

Writers
Susan Blum
Marlene Targ Brill
James I. Clark
Theresa Kryst Fertig
Kathleen L. Florio
Robert Knight
Hortense Leon
Anne V. McGravie
Katie Clark Sharp

Graphics and Design

Senior Art Director
Tom Evans

Coordinator, Design Development and Production
Brenda B. Tropinski

Senior Designer
Isaiah Sheppard

Senior Designer
Matthew Carrington

Media Researcher
Rosalia Bledsoe

Manufacturing/ Production

Production/Technology Manager
Anne Fritzinger

Production Specialist
Curley Hunter

Proofreader
Nathalie Strassheim

World Book, Inc.
180 North LaSalle Street, Suite 900
Chicago, Illinois 60601 USA

For information about other World Book publications, visit our website at **www.worldbook.com** or call **1-800-WORLDBK (967-5325).** For information about sales to schools and libraries, call **1-800-975-3250 (United States); 1-800-837-5365 (Canada).**

The publisher wishes to acknowledge permission for use of materials from the following resource: Betty Glad, *Jimmy Carter, In Search of the Great White House* (New York, 1980), W. W. Norton & Company, Inc.

Printed in China by Shenzhen Donnelley Printing Co., Ltd., Guangdong Province
15th printing January 2017

The Library of Congress has cataloged a previous edition of this title as follows:

The World Book of America's presidents.
  p. cm.
  Includes index.
  Summary: "Examines the United States presidency and its historical importance. Includes biographical information about every U.S. president and information and photos of every first lady. Discusses the duties, privileges, and the broad power of the president, and examines the people who have led the country through times of poverty and prosperity, peace and war"--Provided by publisher.
  ISBN 978-0-7166-3700-4
  1. Presidents--United States. 2. Presidents--United States--Biography. 3. United States--Politics and government.
I. World Book, Inc.
E176.1.W395 2009
973.09'9--dc22

               2008039358

The World Book of America's Presidents: The President's World
This revised edition:
ISBN 978-0-7166-3702-8 (set, hc.)
ISBN 978-0-7166-3703-5 (hc.)

Contents

The President: A Unique Leader

★★★

The President of the United States has been called the most powerful person in the world—and with good reason. In spite of the fact that the framers of the Constitution listed all the powers of the President in just a few paragraphs, the President today occupies a uniquely powerful position. Over the years, events and presidential personalities have molded the office of the presidency, so that the President has become truly a world leader, as well as leader of the nation.

One of the reasons for this position is the variety of roles the President plays in American political life. As chief of state, the President carries out various ceremonial functions, such as greeting foreign dignitaries and hosting glittering state dinners. As the nation's chief executive, the President is responsible for the enforcement of federal laws and can appoint and remove thousands of federal officials. The President shapes the nation's domestic and foreign policies by proposing legislation and issuing executive orders. The President serves as commander-in-chief of the nation's armed forces. In addition, this national leader heads a political party and is expected to give time and support to party affairs. In most other countries, these various functions are carried out by more than one person. But in the United States, they are all the President's responsibility.

At first glance, it might appear that the President, with all these powers, could easily become a dictator. But the U.S. Constitution carefully provides for a "separation of powers" among the three branches of government to avoid just such a situation. The judicial and legislative branches both have powers of their own, some meant to keep the President's powers under control.

The President and Vice-President of the United States are the only U.S. officials elected by voters throughout the nation. Unlike senators or governors or mayors, the President is elected to serve all Americans. Even those who did not vote for the President recognize this elected official as the head of the government. The President stands as the most visible symbol of the nation, both to fellow Americans and to people all over the world.

★★★

Americans look to their President to solve complicated national problems, to lead them through crises, and to set priorities and policies that will affect their everyday lives in many ways. Although the responsibilities for governing the nation are largely in the hands of thousands of elected and appointed officials, it is the President who stands in the spotlight of national attention. When government policies are successful, it is the President who often enjoys the praise and thanks of the nation. But the President is also the person who shoulders much of the blame when government policies fail to produce desired results.

The President owes much of the prominence of the office to a vast communications network that focuses on day-to-day presidential activities. The President can command the attention of millions of Americans—as well as people in other parts of the world—when speaking on television, for example. Television and radio broadcasts and newspaper, Internet, and magazine stories all report on the President's official activities as well as leisure time. When the President travels, reporters from the American and foreign press follow along. The American people can expect to see their President addressing the Congress, greeting foreign dignitaries, signing landmark pieces of legislation, and attending the theater. The President and the rest of the first family quickly become celebrities recognized around the world.

The power and prestige of the presidency are reflected in the various privileges and special services that are available to whoever occupies the White House. Dozens of domestic employees staff the Executive Mansion to ensure the comfort of the President and first family and to assist with the countless social functions that take place there day after day. The presidential limousine commands instant access to even the busiest streets, and a fleet of helicopters stands ready to transport the President on short trips at a moment's notice. The presidential jetliner, Air Force One, provides the President with a luxurious airborne home and office. Communications specialists accompany the President everywhere so that the national leader can be in instant contact with White House staff no matter what the location. Advance teams make the necessary special arrangements for presidential appearances, and Secret Service agents protect the President night and day. Advisers, speechwriters, secretaries, military aides—all contribute to the aura of power and glory that marks the American presidency.

Many people would argue that it is the nature of the United States itself that has made the American President such a unique and powerful leader. The United States is a nation of tremendous diversity—in its landscape, its people, its natural resources, and its economy. It is also one of the most technologically advanced countries in the world, and its industries provide food, manufactured goods, and other products to people all over the globe. The United States is tied to other nations in a complex mesh of trade agreements, defense treaties, foreign-aid pacts, and other mutual arrangements. As a result, many of the decisions made by the President affect people who live far away from the United States.

America's cherished traditions of democracy have guided and supported the presidency from its earliest days. The President of the United States stands at the head of a system of government that is one of the most successful in history. From the time of George Washington to the present day, one President after another has succeeded to the office in a peaceful, orderly manner. Most Presidents were elected to power. But some have assumed office unexpectedly—as the result of the natural death, assassination, or resignation of a President. But even in these times of national crisis, the reins of power have been handed over to the new President in a calm manner, and the business of governing the nation has continued uninterrupted.

Few other nations in the world have enjoyed such stability in their governments. And no other nation can claim a leader with more far-reaching responsibilities than those of the American President.

Introduction

The President's life is a fascinating life, filled with many duties, some privilege, and awesome power. The presidency is in part the product of tradition. Today's President serves the nation from the White House in Washington, D.C. It is the same mansion where all the Presidents except George Washington lived, and which he helped plan. And the President wins the nation's highest office through an election system that slowly evolved and grew in complexity with America.

The President is also the product of the times. George Washington would be astonished at how quickly *Air Force One,* the presidential jet, flies today's President around the world. And, to protect the nation's leader, the Secret Service uses the most sensitive devices modern technology can provide.

Now *The President's World* makes you a part of the unique existence of the President of the United States. "The Story of the Presidency," the first section, shows where the office of President came from, how its powers grew, and how they were sometimes checked. The story of past Presidents becomes the story of the modern presidency in "The President Today," which describes the duties of the most important office in the free world. This section explains the many different roles of the President. It also helps you understand how the executive branch of the government works and who assists the President in ensuring the nation's welfare.

"Destination: Pennsylvania Avenue" will take you on the campaign trail to the presidency. Here, all the steps in the President's election are described, from the statement of candidacy through the primaries, and on to the national political convention, the popular vote in November, and finally the Electoral College vote—the end of a long and difficult path. Inauguration Day takes place in "Moving into the White House." In this section, the President repeats the oath of office in the inspiring ceremony that leads to the historic mansion on the Potomac River: the White House, home of the U.S. President. The mansion is described in detail, and beautiful illustrations give you a first-hand view in this section.

An introduction to the capital of the United States comes next in "Washington: The President's Hometown." Created expressly to be the seat of government, Washington is a city for all America. Visit the imposing Capitol, the impressive monuments, and the incomparable museums and parks while reading this section. Then, learn how the President is protected in the capital and elsewhere in "Guarding the President's Life." Secret Service agents are everywhere in the passages of this section.

In "On the Road with the President," you will learn what it is like to travel presidential style. From the horse and buggy to *Air Force One,* you will ride with the Presidents in whatever vehicles they have used.

This volume ends with a topical index. It is an aid to help you quickly locate the interesting information you want to know about the world of America's Presidents.

The Story of the Presidency

After the Battle of Yorktown in October 1781, George Washington moved his army into camp at Newburgh, N.Y., to await a peace treaty with Great Britain. But as cheering over victory and the prospect of independence faded, the troops' outlook appeared bleak. They had gone without pay for months, with little hope of soon getting the money owed them. The Continental Congress was unable to meet its financial obligations.

The whole country, in fact, was in poor shape economically. Neither money nor jobs seemed available for those veterans ready to shed their tattered uniforms. Adding to their woes, the currency that the Continental Congress issued during the war—paper notes called continentals—had lost so much purchasing power as to make "not worth a continental" an equivalent for worthlessness.

Colonel Lewis Nicola of Pennsylvania concluded that only drastic action could save the army and the country for which he had fought. On May 22, 1782, Nicola wrote in desperation to his commander in chief, General George Washington.

Rally the army, Nicola urged the general. Seize power and declare yourself king. Establish a government strong enough at least to shoulder its financial responsibilities.

Washington was appalled. "With a mixture of great surprise and astonishment," he responded, " I read with attention the sentiments you have submitted to my perusal. Be assured, sir, no occurrence in the course of the war, has given me more painful sensations than your information of there being such ideas existing in the army as you have expressed, and I must view [them] with abhorrence and reprehend with severity.... If I am not deceived in myself, you could not have found a person to whom your schemes were more disagreeable." Washington urged Nicola "to banish these thoughts from your mind, and never communicate ... a sentiment of like nature."

Nicola apologized in a second letter, hastily adding that he would never mention the subject again. He implored Washington not to connect him publicly with such ideas. The general did not.

However, in March 1783, Washington had to deal with the threat of an uprising among his officers, who were still without pay and

discouraged over Congress's lack of action on that issue and on army pensions. Washington persuaded his officers not to rebel, and the crisis within the army passed. The soldiers eventually were paid.

Economic conditions improved little, however, and discontent grew. The government was operating under the Articles of Confederation, adopted in 1781, which provided for no executive office, no authority to tax or regulate trade, and no means for Congress to enforce its will.

Talk of a monarchy increased, too, as Washington noted in a letter to John Jay of New York in 1786: "I am told that even respectable characters speak of a monarchical form of government without horror.... What a triumph for the advocates of despotism to find that we are incapable of governing ourselves.... Would to God that wise measures be taken in time to avert the consequences we have but too much reason to apprehend."

For Washington, Jay, Alexander Hamilton, James Madison, and others, the "wise

Page 10: Paintng of Washington's second inaugural on March 4, 1793.

The Constitution was signed in Independence Hall in Philadelphia on Sept. 17, 1787, after nearly four months of debate.

measures" became a convention in Philadelphia early in 1787. There they and 51 other delegates from 12 states came together to revise the Articles of Confederation. They ended with a new document, the Constitution of the United States.

The Chief Executive

Some sentiment favoring a monarchy existed at Philadelphia, but no member of the convention pushed the idea hard. By September 1787, delegates has agreed on a republican government of three branches—legislative, judicial, and executive—and they vested executive power in a President who would be elected to a four-year term with no limit on eligibility for re-election. The Constitution's writers granted the office of the presidency many powers, but they hedged most with Congressional checks and balances.

The President, for example, could veto bills that any Congress passed. Congress could override a veto with a two-thirds majority vote.

The President would be commander in chief of the armed services, but only Congress could declare war. The President could make treaties with other nations, but no treaty could go into effect until the Senate ratified it. Senate approval was also necessary for presidential appointments to numerous offices. One presidential power went unchecked: "to grant reprieves and pardons for offenses against the United States."

Congress's check on the presidency lay in its power to remove from office any civil officer "on impeachment for, and conviction of, treason, bribery, or other high crimes and misdemeanors." The House of Representatives could vote articles of impeachment—accusations of wrongdoing—and the Senate would try the accused.

The entire structure of the presidency, like other parts of the Constitution, represented compromise. In this case, it was between delegates who favored a "weak" presidency and those who wanted a "strong" one.

Roger Sherman of Connecticut spoke for the "weak" point of view. According to James

Madison, who kept convention notes: "He considered the executive magistracy as nothing more than an institution for carrying the will of the legislature into effect."

Those favoring a "strong" President patterned their thinking on the New York state constitution of 1777. That document provided for a governor elected by the people to a three-year term, with unlimited eligibility for re-election. The governor could also, in conjunction with a council of revision, veto bills the legislature passed. Gouverneur Morris of New York stated the case for a strong executive in this way:

> One great object of the executive is to control the legislature. The legislature will continually seek to strengthen and perpetuate themselves; and will seize those critical moments produced by war, invasion or convulsion for that purpose. It is necessary then that the executive magistrate should be the guardian of the people, even of the lower classes, against legislative tyranny, against the great and the wealthy who in the course of things will necessarily compose the legislative body.

Yet the delegates wrote most presidential powers in vague language, open to interpretation. This has allowed individuals in many instances to fashion the office of the presidency as they saw fit.

As to the vice-presidency, some delegates at Philadelphia believed the office unnecessary, and they had difficulty establishing vice-presidential duties. When it was proposed that the Vice-President be made President of the Senate, Elbridge Gerry of Massachusetts objected. He thought that an unfortunate mixture of executive and legislative functions. On the other hand, according to Madison: "Mr. Sherman saw no danger in the case. If the Vice-President were not to be President of the Senate, he would be without employment." Furthermore, Sherman did not foresee many instances in which the Vice-President would need to act like a legislator and cast a ballot to break a tie vote.

The delegates finally accepted the office, its duty of presiding over the Senate, and its only specified power: that of casting a ballot in the event of a tie vote. And there have been occasions on which the Vice-President has had to vote. But the Vice-President's main function soon became that of remaining a heartbeat away from the presidency. The Constitution as written provided that in case of the removal of the President from office or of death, resignation, or inability to discharge the powers and duties of the office, the same would be transferred to the Vice-President.

Settling on a means to select a President required many compromises. Gouverneur Morris stood at one extreme, favoring direct popular election, as in New York state elections. George Mason of Virginia, on the other hand, thought that providing for election by the people would be like offering a choice of colors to the blind. Charles Pinckney of South Carolina agreed. The people would likely be uninformed, he said, and easily swayed by "active and designing people."

Still, those delegates like Mason who favored election by Congress or by state legislatures could not carry their point, either. Selection by either house of the Congress would make the presidency a creature of the national legislature. Election by the states would grant them too much power over the central government.

The Electoral College compromise did not please anyone at Philadelphia entirely, but most delegates agreed that it was the best they could do under the circumstances. This indirect means of choosing a President contained some part of nearly every proposal placed before the convention, involving the people, the states, and Congress.

Under the Electoral College system, each state was to have as many electors as it had representatives in the House and Senate. The states would determine how they chose the electors, and each elector would vote for two persons. The candidate receiving the greatest number of votes, provided that number was a majority of the total number of electors, would become President and the runner-up would become Vice-President. In case of a tie vote for the presidency, or failure of one person to receive a majority of electoral votes, the House of Representatives, with each state represented casting one ballot, would elect the President, with the runner-up becoming Vice-President. In case of a runner-up tie, the Senate would elect the Vice-President.

At first, some state legislatures chose electors. But this gradually changed to allow citizens to cast ballots directly for those who in turn would vote for President.

Delegates to the Constitutional Convention left Philadelphia in September 1787, confident

Washington and his Cabinet are pictured in an 1876 print by Currier & Ives. The Cabinet includes (from left to right): Secretary of War Henry Knox; Secretary of the Treasury Alexander Hamilton; Secretary of State Thomas Jefferson; and Attorney General Edmund Randolf.

that George Washington would be the first President of the United States. They, and Americans in general, believed that the nation would be in good hands. And in the first election, in 1789, all electors cast a ballot for Washington. John Adams received the second highest number out of a total of 12 candidates and became Vice-President.

The First President

Washington was deeply aware that almost every one of his acts would set a precedent. Above all, he wished to cloak the presidency with dignity, and this suited Washington's personality. Relaxed among close friends, he tended to be formal in public.

To avoid being plagued by visitors—as he was at first—Washington held regular Tuesday levees, or receptions, for men only. But he was criticized for copying a custom that European monarchs followed. The affairs remained formal, but not so ceremonious after the first one.

On that occasion Washington's aide, David Humphreys, assembled the guests and then shouted: "The President of the United States!" as Washington entered the room. Washington was startled and shaken, and later he told his aide that he would not allow himself to be introduced in that manner again. And so the story of the presidency began.

Washington established the first group of advisers, now called the Cabinet. It was within the Cabinet that American political party leadership developed, much to his distress. Thomas Jefferson, the secretary of state, held a point of view that was shared by rural Americans and others who wanted to preserve the powers of the state. He was a "strict constructionist," one who believed that federal powers were limited to those expressly stated in the Constitution. Secretary of the Treasury Alexander Hamilton upheld the idea of constitutionally implied power, as that found in what is called the "elastic clause" in Article I, Section 8. This grants Congress the right "to make all laws which shall be necessary and proper for carrying into execution the foregoing powers, and all other powers vested by this Constitution in the government of the United States, or in any department or officer thereof." Jefferson's ideas formed the basis for the Democratic-Republican Party, while Hamilton's characterized the Federalist Party.

Jefferson and Hamilton clashed many times. For example, they differed over the Bank of the United States, which Congress established in 1791. Hamilton urged President Washington to sign the bill, assuring him that Congress had the power to create such an institution. Jefferson pointed out the absence of any specific authorization for a national bank in the Constitution. Washington followed Hamilton's advice.

Quarreling within the Cabinet led to Jefferson's resignation in 1793. Hamilton left in January 1795. Washington soon had an entirely new advisory group and, as it turned out, one with a unanimous Federalist point of view, ensuring partisan advice. At the same time, Washington continued to rely on Hamilton, now in private life. Without meaning to, for he detested the idea of political parties, Washington had set the precedent of a President filling Cabinet seats with political supporters.

George Washington established the President as the chief author of foreign policy when he declared the United States neutral during war between France and Great Britain in the 1790's. Jefferson's followers believed that the 1778 treaty with France, which had brought the United States much-needed aid during the Revolution, obligated the nation to support France now. Although favoring Britain, Hamilton's people upheld neutrality. And despite criticism, Washington made his policy stick. In 1794, Congress enacted a neutrality law.

Washington set yet another precedent when he refused to consider a third term in 1796. After that, no President ran for more until Franklin D. Roosevelt in 1940.

One precedent Washington may have hoped to create did not work out. Instead of accepting a salary, he asked Congress simply to meet the expenses of the presidency. Washington had followed a similar course while commander in chief of the Continental Army, accepting expense money but no pay. Congress refused. Instead, it voted the President $25,000 annually, out of which the office's expenses would be paid. Washington had difficulty meeting expenses on his salary. John Adams, on the other hand, saved money from his. The President's salary remained at $25,000 until the Ulysses S. Grant Administration in the 1870's. Then, amid public howls of protest over the "salary grab," Congress doubled the amount, at the same time increasing its members' pay.

The clause in the Constitution that directs the President to "take care that the laws be faithfully executed" came home to Washington in 1794 with the Whiskey Rebellion. At issue was a federal excise tax on hard liquor. Congress had imposed the tax in 1791 to help pay war debts.

Because of the poor transportation system in their region, farmers in North Carolina, western Pennsylvania, and Virginia pre-

Do You Know?
1. What was the salary of the early Presidents?
2. What did Thomas Jefferson refer to as the "pest of the peace of the world"?
3. What war was known as "Mr. Madison's War"?
4. Who referred to the presidency as a "bully pulpit"?
5. Who is called the first "log-cabin" President?
6. What was the "Revolution of 1800"?
7. What President was called "His Rotundity"?
8. How were the first presidential candidates nominated?
9. What state never sent a delegate to the Constitutional Convention?
10. What are "His Mightiness," "His Elective Majesty," and "His Elective Highness"?

Answers: (1) $25,000, until Grant; (2) diplomacy; (3) the War of 1812; (4) T. Roosevelt; (5) Jackson; (6) Jefferson's election—a Democratic-Republican win over a Federalist regime; (7) J. Adams, as Vice-President; (8) Congressional caucus; (9) Rhode Island; (10) titles debated in Congress before the plain address, "Mr. President," was chosen for the Chief Executive.

ferred to turn bulky corn and rye into liquid in stills before hauling it to market. Whiskey was easier to transport, and it also fetched a good price and profit, which the federal excise tax cut into. At first, Western farmers were content to protest the levy in petitions to Congress. Later, they roughed up tax collectors, burned the stills of those who paid the tax, and interfered with the mails and with court proceedings against violators of the law.

President Washington decided on strong action. Calling on the governors of Maryland, Virginia, New Jersey, and Pennsylvania for troops, the President made himself commander in chief in fact as well as in name. Washington assembled about 13,000 soldiers. He sent them westward from Philadelphia, then the nation's capital, turning command over to General Henry Lee. The rebellion quickly petered out, and Lee's troops marched a number of "Whiskey Boys" through December rain and mud to Philadelphia.

All were eventually placed on trial, but only two rebels were found guilty—one of mail robbery and the other of participating in a riot in Fayette Co., Pa. After having fulfilled his duty to enforce the law, Washington now used his pardoning power. He released the two.

Not all his acts as President were approved unanimously, and the criticism he endured did not set well with Washington. Still, no President has departed the office with the nearly universal admiration and respect he enjoyed. When he retired to Mount Vernon in March 1797, George Washington left behind a government firmly established.

Politics and Presidents

Although Washington was unanimously elected President twice, party politics had begun to influence the Electoral College by the end of his second term. All electors did not as yet follow strict party lines, however, as the election of 1796 demonstrated.

That year John Adams of Massachusetts and Thomas Pinckney of South Carolina were Federalist candidates, while Thomas Jefferson of Virginia and Aaron Burr of New York formed the Democratic-Republican ticket. The electors chose Adams President, but enough voted for Jefferson to make him Vice-President.

John Marshall served as chief justice of the United States from 1801 to 1835.

The electoral system took yet another twist four years later, when Jefferson and Burr, both representing the same party again, wound up tied. After 36 ballots, the House of Representatives finally settled on Jefferson, which made Burr Vice-President.

That election led to the 12th Amendment to the Constitution, which went into effect in 1804. Henceforth, the Electoral College would choose a President and a Vice-President on separate ballots.

Jefferson, re-elected in 1804, brought an informal style to the presidency. As one writer of the time said, he was "an enemy to luxury.... He lives at Monticello in the simple and negligent style of a man wholly devoted to rural philosophical pursuits."

Jefferson behaved much the same in the presidency. He walked from his boarding house in Washington, D.C., to the Capitol on Inauguration Day in 1801. His office was always open to visitors. And although historians on the whole have not given Jefferson consistently high marks as President, none has faulted his Louisiana Purchase. He got much more than he sought.

Jefferson had set out to obtain only the mouth of the Mississippi River, the area around New Orleans. He wanted this to ensure an outlet to the sea and world markets for Western farmers, who wished to ship produce down the Ohio and Mississippi rivers. But Napoleon Bonaparte of France, who had obtained Louisiana from Spain, offered to sell the entire territory.

Napoleon's proposal embarrassed Jefferson, a strict constructionist. He could find nothing in the Constitution authorizing the purchase of such a vast area. New Englanders objected on other grounds—they feared that the acquisition of additional land would dilute their region's political and economic influence when the new land began to fill with people.

Few members of Congress raised objections, though, and Jefferson's doubts about the legality of the purchase soon faded. As a consequence, enough land was added to double the size of the United States at a cost of a few cents an acre or hectare.

Perhaps no President has managed Congress with greater skill than Jefferson. He never exercised his veto during his entire presidency. Of the early Presidents in fact, all had few or no vetoes in office—the first 10 Presidents had only 33 vetoes among them. By comparison, Jimmy Carter had 31 vetoes, a fairly usual amount for a modern President, but only 2 fewer vetoes than the first 10 Presidents combined.

A Strong Executive

Andrew Jackson, the first Democrat to be elected President, applied his most famous veto in 1832 against a bill to recharter the Bank of the United States. The bank, established in 1791, had withstood all constitutional challenges, but Jackson opposed it and he had no use for its president, Nicholas Biddle. Jackson believed that the bank possessed too much power and that it was opposed to the interests of farming and small business. He was convinced that a President could exercise the veto on policy as well as constitutional grounds.

Biddle and the bank's supporters, most of them members of the Whig Party, intensely disliked Jackson. "The bank, Mr. Van Buren," Jackson declared to the one who would succeed him in 1837, "is trying to kill me, but I will kill it!" And kill it he did, with a stinging veto denouncing the institution. Congress failed to override the veto in 1832.

Jackson moved in 1833 to have the federal funds on deposit in the bank withdrawn and placed in state institutions that Jackson's enemies quickly dubbed "pet banks." When Secretary of the Treasury William Duane refused to carry out Jackson's orders, as under law he could, the President fired him. Jackson then appointed Roger Taney treasury secretary and Taney gradually arranged for the withdrawals.

The Senate had not been in session when Jackson appointed Taney, and that body refused to confirm him as secretary of the treasury. The Senate went on to censure Jackson for having taken "upon himself authority and power not conferred by the Constitution and laws, but in derogation of both." The President dismissed the censure as unconstitutional.

Jackson's personal feelings also led him to ignore a decision made by the Supreme Court of the United States that did not suit him. In the 1830's, white citizens of Georgia wished to take over land owned and farmed by the Cherokee Indian Nation. The Georgia legislature passed laws affecting the Indian lands. However, the Supreme Court ruled in 1832 that the federal government, not the states, had authority over Indian lands. Jackson, who had made a name fighting Indians, sympathized with the Georgians and believed that the Indians should move out.

The executive branch, with Jackson at its head, had authority to enforce the nation's laws, not the courts. The Cherokee stood no chance. The U.S. Army moved them off their land and forced them onto reservations west of the Mississippi.

Historians generally do not applaud Andrew Jackson's attitude toward the Cherokee, and many doubt the wisdom of his destroying the bank instead of simply trying to curb its power. But most historians praise Jackson for facing down South Carolina during the nullification controversy of the early 1830's.

Protesting a tariff law which many Southerners opposed, South Carolina in November 1832 declared that a state had the

Oliver Hazard Perry at the Battle of Lake Erie during the War of 1812, dubbed "Mr. Madison's War" by critics.

right to nullify a federal statute and resolved that the law was not in force within its boundaries. It threatened to secede, or leave the Union, if the government tried to collect the taxes involved. "The laws of the United States must be executed," Jackson declared, and he sent troops and warships to the Charleston area. Jackson demanded, and Congress passed, a force bill that authorized the President to use the armed forces to collect tariffs. However, a compromise tariff measure was quickly passed, and South Carolina withdrew its nullification ordinance.

Andrew Jackson was a strong President because he was a forceful one and a majority of the voters supported him. Jackson, in fact, was the first President to proclaim that only he represented all the people, in contrast to Congress, whose members represented states and districts within states. Some Presidents who defied Congress and the Supreme Court would be less successful.

Whether John Tyler was one of those can be debated. At heart a Democrat and referred to as "His Accidency" because he became President upon William Henry Harrison's death in 1841, Tyler enjoyed neither popular support nor that of the Whig Party, under whose banner he had run with Harrison. Many people doubted that Tyler should be more than "acting President" until a new election was held.

William Henry Harrison was the first President to die in office. The constitutional phrase covering the situation, stating that the "powers and duties" of the President "shall devolve on the Vice-President," was being interpreted for the first time, and it was vague.

Whether constitutionally temporary or not, Tyler acted like a President, and he vetoed such Whig-sponsored legislation as that establishing a new national bank. The best the Whig-controlled House could do was censure Tyler, who was not nominated for the presidency in 1844.

The year 1844 was a Democratic year, and James K. Polk won the presidency running on a platform calling for the nation's expansion. Polk was especially interested in acquiring California, then held by Mexico. But he could not persuade the Mexican government to sell the territory, so he turned to other means, including promoting rebellion against Mexican authorities in California.

In addition, there was the Texas boundary question. The United States claimed that the border lay along the Rio Grande. Mexico insisted that it was the Nueces River, farther north.

Polk sent General Zachary Taylor with a detachment of troops into the disputed area in March 1846, and the inevitable incident occurred—Americans were fired upon and some were killed. Polk asked Congress to declare war, and it did so on May 13, 1846. In the Mexican War, the United States obtained California, New Mexico, and the Rio Grande region.

Civil War President

Abraham Lincoln, a member of Congress from Illinois, opposed the Mexican War and called on Polk to point to the place on American soil where the initial shooting incident had taken place. Years later, Lincoln found himself a war President and, during the opening weeks of the Civil War especially, he ruled like a dictator. After the Confederate bombardment of Fort Sumter in April 1861, Lincoln did not call Congress into special session until July. In the meantime, he used powers as commander in chief—and not always within constitutional limits.

Having responded to what he considered an attack on the United States, Lincoln defended his actions before Congress when it assembled on July 4: "These measures," he said, "whether strictly legal or not, were ventured upon, under what appeared to be popular demand and a public necessity, trusting … that Congress would readily ratify them. It is believed that nothing has been done beyond the constitutional competency of Congress." And Congress endorsed Lincoln's policies with appropriate legislation, including the suspension of habeas corpus.

The Emancipation Proclamation itself went beyond normal presidential authority because the Constitution protected slavery and the Fifth Amendment prohibits depriving any citizen of property without due process of law. Lincoln

regarded the proclamation as a war measure, and he later supported the 13th Amendment to the Constitution, which abolished slavery in the United States.

Faced with an unprecedented situation, Lincoln's first and enduring impulse was to save the Union, which by definition also meant the Constitution. Few historians have found fault with his actions and as one put it: "The American people will gag down strong medicines for critical national ills."

Abraham Lincoln was neither the first nor the last President to use police and commander-in-chief powers in what some people regarded as high-handed ways. Polk had. So had Thomas Jefferson, against the Barbary States in the early 1800's.

Pirates infested the Mediterranean Sea, operating out of Morocco, Algiers, and Tripoli to prey on merchant vessels. U.S. policy had been to negotiate treaties with what were called the Barbary States, which controlled the marauders, and pay tribute for safe passage. Jefferson followed this policy, but at one point he ordered a naval squadron heading for the Mediterranean Sea that if the Barbary States declared war on the United States, the squadron was free to destroy their ships wherever they might be found. Tripoli declared war, and the U.S.S. *Enterprise* sank a pirate vessel. Jefferson then asked Congress for authority to order American ships to defend themselves, neglecting to mention that he had already given the order to fire. Congress complied.

About 100 years later, President Theodore Roosevelt wanted the United States to take over rights that Colombia had granted a French company to build a canal through Panama, then part of Colombia. Roosevelt found the Colombian price too high, however, and use other means to obtain an American canal.

With U.S. encouragement, Panamanians staged a revolution and declared their independence in November 1903. To prevent Colombia from sending troops to put down the uprising, Roosevelt stationed a U.S. warship off the Panamanian coast. "I took Panama," Roosevelt is said to have boasted as the United States recognized the region's independence. America got its canal but earned resentment from Latin Americans.

Theodore Roosevelt also took it upon himself to declare what is called the "corollary" to the Monroe Doctrine, which warned

An engraving, View of the Capitol at Washington, *shows Pennsylvania Avenue in 1827, with the Capitol in the background.*

European powers against interfering with nations in the Western Hemisphere. In 1904, Roosevelt stated: "Chronic wrongdoing, or an impotence which results in a general loosening of the ties of a civilized society, may in America, as elsewhere, ultimately require intervention by some civilized nation, and in the Western Hemisphere the adherence of the United States to the Monroe Doctrine may force the United States, however reluctantly, in flagrant cases of such wrongdoing or impotence, to the exercise of an international police power." Over the years, on presidential orders, the United States intervened in Cuba, Nicaragua, the Dominican Republic, and Haiti—to restore order or to collect debts those nations owed European powers.

In 1914, President Woodrow Wilson sent naval vessels and marines to Vera Cruz, Mexico, seeking to throw U.S. weight against Victoriano Huerta, who had seized power and then faced a rebellion. Huerta eventually fell after fighting in Vera Cruz, but many nations condemned the United States for interfering in the affairs of another country.

Wilson later dispatched cavalry forces into northern Mexico to try to bring to bay the bandit Pancho Villa, who had led his band in raids during which some Americans were killed. The troops never found him.

World War Presidents

During World War I, Wilson exercised great power as President, much as Lincoln had in the Civil War—with Congressional and, for the most part, public approval. Wilson allowed the American Protective League to operate, which at its peak had some 250,000 members in about 600 communities. The league took on the task of ferreting out draft dodgers and others with "unpatriotic" leanings. So many accusations of breaking and entering and intimidation fell upon the organ-ization that Wilson finally put an end to it.

With the beginning of World War II in September 1939, President Franklin D. Roosevelt believed that U.S. interests lay in supporting the Allies against Germany and Italy, and he moved cautiously to bring public opinion behind that point of view. This became easier after France fell and Great Britain was left to fight Germany alone. Most Americans, while not wanting the United States to enter the war, had been pro-British from the beginning.

On his own, Roosevelt made an agreement with Great Britain to exchange 50 over-age U.S. destroyers for the right to use bases on British-held territory in the Atlantic Ocean. As commander in chief, he ordered U.S. troops to Iceland in 1941 and, after a U.S. destroyer had been torpedoed by a German submarine, Roosevelt issued orders for U.S. warships to "shoot on sight" German submarines active in the Atlantic. All this occurred before the United States was at war officially.

Roosevelt's exercise of presidential power before and during World War II mirrored his activist approach in domestic affairs in the 1930's. His ambitious New Deal programs brought many reforms to the federal government and broadly extended government intervention in the economy to assist people suffering from the effects of the Great Depression.

The United States entered World War II on Dec. 7, 1941, when Japan attacked Pearl Harbor, Hawaii, which was at that time an American territory. The attack prompted an immediate declaration of war by the U.S. Congress. President Roosevelt used powers Congress voted him, or those left over from World War I, to conduct the war. As with World War I, during World War II the President exercised considerable statutory authority over American industry as well as over other aspects of the war effort. It was an executive order, on the other hand, not legislation passed by Congress, that led to Japanese-Americans on the Pacific Coast being rounded up and shipped to internment camps in the interior.

President Roosevelt died on April 12, 1945, and was succeeded by Vice-President Harry S. Truman. Roosevelt's death left Truman with the responsibility of bringing World War II to a successful conclusion and the challenge of building a postwar peace. President Truman made one of the most important presidential decisions in history when he ordered a terrible new weapon, the atomic bomb, to be used against the Japanese cities of Hiroshima and Nagasaki in August 1945. These events prompted the surrender of Japan and the end of World War II. Truman also participated in the founding of the United Nations (UN) in 1945.

Expanded Presidential Powers

Presidents typically exercise expanded powers during wartime, then return to a less dominant role in the federal government when peace returns. This did not happen after World War II. Soon after the defeat of Japan and Germany, the Soviet Union, the world's leading Communist power, embraced an aggressive, expansionist policy in Europe and Asia. The need to challenge Soviet aggression kept the United States on military alert and a partial war footing. The Cold War had begun.

During the early part of the Cold War, from the late 1940's to the mid-1970's, Presidents responded quickly to international threats, particularly from Communist nations, often without the approval of Congress. Because Presidents projected American military force throughout the world with relatively little oversight from Congress, the Cold War era came to be known by some as the era of the imperial presidency.

The first "hot war"—or outright shooting war—of the Cold War was the Korean War. The conflict began in June 1950, when Communist North Korea invaded U.S.-backed South Korea. In response, President Harry Truman sent U.S. forces based in Japan to Korea to meet the invasion. Truman obtained a resolution from the UN Security Council (central governing body) condemning North Korea's invasion and authorizing member nations to send troops in support of South Korea. Nevertheless, the bulk of the war effort fell on the United States.

The Korean War dragged on for three years as fortunes of the two sides rose and fell. In April 1951, President Truman dismissed General Douglas MacArthur from command in Korea after the general criticized the administration's war policy. Truman's action reaffirmed presidential power as commander in chief in wartime. Truman's Administration was unable, however, to bring an end to the hot war in Korea. That fell to Truman's successor, President Dwight D. Eisenhower, in 1953. The war ended in a cease-fire stalemate after the death of more than 36,000 American troops and many thousands more of Korean and other nationalities.

President Eisenhower continued the pattern of strong presidential leadership in the Cold-War struggle. He prompted the Central Intelligence Agency (CIA) to take action against Guatemala and Iran. Both nations were suspected of having governments sponsored by Communist nations. The CIA actions resulted in the overthrow of both governments in the mid-1950's. Eisenhower also committed U.S. advisers to help the government of South Vietnam resist aggression by Communist North Vietnam.

The Cold War came to a dangerous and frightening period in the early 1960's. Revolutionary leader Fidel Castro had taken control of Cuba in 1959, declared himself a Communist two years later, and opened the country to Soviet influence and military presence. In October 1962, U.S. aircraft revealed the presence in Cuba of missiles capable of carrying nuclear warheads. The target of any such weapons appeared to be obvious—the United States, which was Cuba's mainland neighbor immediately to the north. President John F. Kennedy, with the military might and nuclear arsenal of the United States at his beckoning, demanded that the Soviets withdraw their missiles from Cuba. He enforced the demand by imposing a blockade on the island, surrounding it with U.S. warships prepared to attack. To the great relief of most of the world, the Soviet leaders removed the missiles. Soviet premier Nikita

Khrushchev, however, paid the price for his loss of face, losing his job to Kremlin opponents two years later.

Kennedy's successor, Lyndon B. Johnson, wielded for a time the greatest power of any President since Franklin Roosevelt. Johnson committed the United States to a major war on behalf of the South Vietnamese government, which continued to resist a Communist insurgency sponsored by North Vietnam. Following alleged attacks by Communist forces (known as Viet Cong) on U.S. naval vessels off the coast of North Vietnam in August 1964, Johnson obtained a resolution from Congress authorizing his Administration to repel attacks against U.S. armed forces. Johnson used the resolution as a legal basis for expanded U.S. involvement in the Vietnam War, though it fell short of a declaration of war.

Before controversy over the war overwhelmed Johnson's Administration, however, the President continued the mandate Kennedy and the Democratic Party had won in the 1960 election to pass sweeping domestic legislation. Among these laws were the Civil Rights Act of 1964, the Voting Rights Act of 1965, and Medicare, a program that provides health insurance to the elderly (1965).

Andrew Jackson travels to Washington for his inaugural in 1829. He was considered the first "people's" President.

By 1968, the Johnson Administration had authorized a buildup of U.S. forces to more than one-half million troops in Vietnam. With no end in sight and mounting protest at home, Johnson decided not to run for reelection in 1968. Richard M. Nixon, the Republican candidate, faced Democratic candidate Hubert Humphrey; Nixon won the presidency in the 1968 election and inherited the Vietnam War. Nixon continued military pressure on North Vietnam and authorized raids into neighboring Cambodia.

In early 1973, the Nixon Administration arranged a cease-fire agreement with the governments of the two Vietnams, bringing American involvement to an end. For South Vietnam, however, the ultimate outcome was its surrender to Communist rebels and North Vietnamese troops in April 1975.

To many observers, Nixon was a President who made full use of his powers. Not only did he extend presidential powers in foreign affairs, he—or aides acting on his behalf—attempted to neutralize certain domestic opponents by extralegal methods. One of these attempts, the break-in, burglary, and bugging of Democratic National Committee headquarters in the Watergate office buildings in Washington, D.C., in June of 1972, would eventually bring down Nixon's presidency.

In his 1972 campaign for reelection, President Nixon, a Republican, had faced Democratic Senator George McGovern. Some Nixon aides apparently decided that breaking into Democratic headquarters might yield information that would damage the Democratic presidential campaign. The Watergate break-in became the Watergate affair and dominated domestic politics in 1973 and 1974. Despite the fact that President Nixon had won reelection in a stunning landslide in November 1972, he was brought to the verge of impeachment in Congress in the summer of 1974. Rather than face impeachment, Nixon resigned as President on August 9, 1974. He was the first President to resign his office. Nixon was succeeded by Vice-President Gerald R. Ford.

Nixon's successors, Ford, Jimmy Carter, Ronald Reagan, and George H. W. Bush, continued to exercise their presidential powers. Reagan was a popular President whose landslide election in 1980 represented a swing of the political pendulum to the right, or a more conservative political philosophy. In the mid-1980's, aides of President Reagan secretly sold arms to Iran in a deal designed to obtain release of hostages taken by Islamic radicals in Lebanon. The Reagan administration then used money from these sales to aid "contra" (anti-Communist) rebels in Nicaragua. Both of these actions—the weapon sales to Iran and extending aid to the contras—were prohibited by U.S. law. Congress in 1987 strongly criticized these Reagan policies, which became known as the "Iran-contra affair."

By the late 1980's, the dynamics of the Cold War were changing. Policies of Soviet leader Mikhail Gorbachev and the deepening economic crisis in the Soviet Union caused the so-called Communist bloc in Eastern Europe to begin breaking apart. Popular movements led to the collapse of Communist control in Hungary, Czechoslovakia, Poland, and other nations of Eastern Europe. In 1991, Communist power collapsed in the Soviet Union itself. The next year, Russia and the United States declared the Cold War was over.

Into a New Century

Bill Clinton, a Democrat, became President in 1993. Clinton came to the presidency with ambitious proposals for domestic programs, but he was held in check by a 1994 Republican takeover of Congress.

In 1998, Clinton was impeached for perjury and obstruction of justice. It was the first impeachment of a President since that of Andrew Johnson in 1868. The House of Representatives charged Clinton with lying to a grand jury that was investigating an extramarital affair he had while in office. Other charges included hindering the investigation by encouraging others to lie and conceal evidence on his behalf. The Senate acquitted Clinton in 1999.

The Clinton impeachment took place within a broader context of bitter political divisions in the United States. So-called culture wars pitted largely rural, religious conservatives against secular, urban liberals. Such social issues as abortion and gay rights heightened activism among cultural "warriors."

The election of 2000 came at the height of the culture wars. In that election, George W. Bush, son of former President George H. W. Bush, won a contested victory in the Electoral College while losing the popular vote. The second President Bush was sworn in on Jan. 20, 2001. On September 11 of that year, the United States suffered the worst terrorist attack in its history. On that day, hijacked commercial airplanes were deliberately crashed into the two towers of the World Trade Center in New York City and into the Pentagon near Washington, D.C. Another hijacked jet crashed in Pennsylvania.

Congress and President Bush responded to the terrorist threat by invading Afghanistan in October 2001. The goal was to remove the Taliban, the fundamentalist Islamic government that had harbored al-Qa`ida terrorists who had carried out the September 11 attacks. Congress also enacted the Patriot Act, which gave federal agents expanded powers of investigation in the fight against terrorism.

In March 2003, a U.S.-led coalition invaded Iraq and overthrew dictator Saddam Hussein. The power of the presidency, as during other wars, appeared to expand in the early 2000's. But continued political division in the United States and controversy over the administration's antiterrorist policies made long-term prospects for such expansion uncertain. Bush was reelected in 2004, but he left office with presidential approval ratings among the lowest in history. The unpopular wars in Iraq and Afghanistan continued throughout his administration. In addition, a severe economic crisis marred his final months in office.

In 2008, voters made history when they elected Barack Obama, a U.S. senator from Illinois, the first African American president of the United States. He defeated John McCain, a Republican from Arizona. Obama had defeated Hillary Rodham Clinton, a U.S. senator from New York and former first lady, to win the Democratic nomination. Obama later nominated Hillary Clinton as U.S. secretary of state.

Obama took office as the nation was experiencing its worst economic crisis since the Great Depression of the 1930's. In 2009, he signed a nearly $800-billion economic stimulus bill to shore up an economy reeling from high unemployment and slumping financial markets. In 2010, he signed a historic health insurance reform act that extended coverage to millions of uninsured Americans.

Keeping a promise he had made during the presidential campaign, Obama withdrew all U.S. combat troops from Iraq by the end of August 2010. By December 2011, soldiers who had remained to train Iraqi forces had left as well. In Afghanistan, Obama increased the number of U.S. troops to counter a growing number of Taliban attacks. As attacks in

President-elect Donald Trump meets with President Barack Obama at the White House in November 2016. The transition of power between presidents begins shortly after the national election results are finalized.

Afghanistan decreased, he began to bring most of the troops home.

In April 2011, Obama approved an operation to kill Osama bin Laden, the head of al-Qa`ida. In May, a team of Navy SEALs shot and killed bin Laden during a raid on his compound in Pakistan. Obama called the death of bin Laden "the most significant achievement to date" in the effort to defeat al-Qa`ida.

The economic crisis Obama inherited continued throughout his first term. Efforts to pass legislation to deal with the crisis were hindered by a divided Congress. Although Democrats controlled the Senate, Republicans had won control of the House of Representatives during the 2010 midterm elections. In 2012, Obama defeated Republican Mitt Romney, former governor of Massachusetts, to win reelection.

A Republican takeover of the Senate in 2014 meant that Obama faced insurmountable congressional obstacles to all of his legislative proposals. He relied on the power of the presidency to move forward on a number of issues. Overseas, the administration pursued a nuclear treaty with Iran and levied sanctions against Russian officials following Russian provocations in Ukraine. Domestically, Obama took executive action to protect millions of undocumented immigrants from deportation. A group of 26 states sued to block the measure, however.

In 2016, Republican businessman Donald Trump defeated Democrat Hillary Rodham Clinton to succeed Obama as president. Obama enjoyed high approval ratings as he prepared to leave office in January 2017.

The President Today

The President of the United States is often considered the most powerful elected official in the world. As leader of a nation of great wealth and military strength, the President plays an important role in shaping world events.

What the President thinks, says, and does affects everyone throughout the world. And the President's job is unique. Like a king or queen, the President is chief of state. Like a prime minister, the chief executive heads the U.S. government and conducts foreign policy. Like a general, the President is commander in chief of the armed forces.

In addition, the President proposes legislation to Congress and heads a major political par-ty. No wonder President Harry Truman kept a sign on his desk that read: "The Buck Stops Here."

The U.S. President today is the center of attention of the media of both the United States and the rest of the world. Presidential words and actions are repeated around the globe on radio, on television, on the Internet, and in newspapers and magazines in hundreds of languages. In most other countries, the name and face of the President of the United States is as familiar to the people as the names and faces of their own leaders. The President is truly a world leader as well as the leader of the U.S. government.

As powerful as the role of President of the United States is, however, there are limits to what the President can do. The Constitution establishes a strict separation of powers among the executive, legislative, and judicial branches of the federal government. The President cannot directly control the Congress or the courts. And these branches of the government can limit the President's ability to act.

Probably the greatest limitation on the President's power resides in the people. Every four years, the voters choose their President. The President and the Vice-President are the only public officials in the United States elected on a nationwide basis. In a sense, the President represents all the people, and their opinion counts. Only with the confidence of the people can the President perform the most important role of office—that of leadership.

The President's many different and important duties are performed by more than one

Page 26: The White House Cabinet Room—site of executive decisions.

official in other countries. These duties can be roughly organized into seven roles.

As *chief of state*, the President conducts ceremonial affairs, as royalty would do in nations ruled by monarchies. The President presides at ceremonies at home and travels to other countries on state visits.

The President's duties as *chief executive* are many. The President is responsible for assuring that all federal laws are enforced. In this role, the President exercises emergency powers, shapes and determines policy, nominates officials to serve in the federal government, and runs the executive branch of the government, among other responsibilities.

PEACE   FATHER of his COUNTRY   TEACHER

In a 1907 cartoon, Theodore Roosevelt picks from many roles that were part of his public image.

As *foreign policy director*, the President shares the duty of making foreign policy with Congress. But the President holds the most important position in international affairs.

As *commander in chief* of the armed forces, the President is responsible for national defense in peace or war. This post symbolizes the supremacy of civilian authority over military authority in the United States.

The President as *legislative leader* proposes new laws for Congressional consideration and urges the Congress to act on the proposals. Presidential success has varied in this role, as it has in the President's role as *political leader*. Presidents use this position as head of their political party to influence members of Congress in taking stands on foreign and domestic issues. Legislators, however, owe loyalty to state and local party organizations and to the voters who must re-elect them. They may vote against a bill favored by the President if it meets with opposition at home.

That the President is a *popular leader*—in the public eye—is evidenced by the mail the White House receives: 6,000 pieces each day on the average. President Clinton was the first President with an electronic mail address. He received about 5,000 e-mail messages each day. *Popular* in this sense means "well known" rather than "well liked." The mail, postal and electronic, is both critical and supportive.

The President cannot possibly handle all the many duties of the office without assistance. The Vice-President, with the active support of the President, can exert influence. The Cabinet, usually thought of as the heads of the executive-level departments, varies in influence as an advisory body to the President. But the smooth operation of the departments is critical, and the heads of these departments can be highly influential.

The Executive Office of the President consists of staff agencies that provide the President with information, ideas, and advice. These agencies include the Office of Management and Budget (OMB), the White House Office, and the National Security Council.

Chief of State

Though brief descriptions of the President's roles are useful for understanding the office, they do not show the complexity of the responsibilities the presidency entails. In addition, the roles of the President frequently interweave; therefore, it is difficult to describe a President acting, say, as chief of state without mentioning presidential actions with regard to another role.

In the 1700's, when the Founding Fathers designed the U.S. President's job, monarchy was the style throughout the world. Wishing to avoid any suggestion of monarchy, the writers of the Constitution made the chief of state the chief executive as well. They called this person the President, and U.S. history has shown a successful mix of the two positions.

Specifically, as chief of state, the President receives ambassadors and other foreign representatives, negotiates with foreign powers, and presides over formal occasions in and out of the White House. The chief of state also delivers the annual State of the Union address and many other speeches in person or over radio and television.

Since Franklin Roosevelt's time, Presidents have often journeyed outside the United States as chiefs of state for international conferences. This is called personal presidential diplomacy. This type of personal diplomacy will also be discussed in connection with the President's role as foreign policy director.

The chief of state role requires numerous minor duties. The President lights the White House Christmas tree, proclaims Thanksgiv-

Truman as commander in chief meets with General MacArthur at Wake Island, 1950.

ing and countless other "days," attends fund-raisers, and, since the early 1900's, has usually thrown the first ball to open the baseball season in the spring.

Some of these are significant—to say nothing of privileged—functions, and the respect the President commands as chief of state reinforces the chief executive role. On the other hand, the position as chief of state is restraining. The President is always in the public eye, as is the rest of the first family.

The public notes everything a President and members of the first family do or say. To the American public, little about a President is sacred, chief of state or no, even with a popular hero like Dwight D. Eisenhower. The surgeon who operated on Ike to correct abdominal problems in 1957 conducted a lengthy press conference at which he described the procedure in detail with the aid of a diagram representing the presidential intestines.

Still, there is much grandeur in the ceremonies that involve the chief of state. And the

President Barack Obama speaks at a state dinner held in honor of visiting Chinese President Hu Jintao at the White House in January 2011.

President spends an estimated 15 to 20 percent of the term of office participating in ceremonial events. President Gerald Ford questioned this much investment but added that if these "activities are not done, the public gets the wrong impression of the President."

Ford met with his White House press secretary each day to relay information to reporters. He also made regular public appearances at dinners, fund-raisers, and press conferences.

Part of the presidential greeting to foreign dignitaries is a formal welcome following the arrival. On the White House front lawn, an honor guard and color guard line the driveway as the visitor's car approaches. Throngs of government officials invited by ticket mill around in anticipation of the full military ceremony. A state dinner is called when another chief of state, such as a president or queen, is visiting, and an official dinner signals a prime minister as a guest of honor.

When the President travels as a chief of state, formalities are observed according to protocol in the foreign land. Sometimes the first lady, a Cabinet member, or other person designated by the President may fill in if the traveling chief executive's schedule is packed. At other times, a "substitute" travels alone.

Perhaps the most stirring ceremonies the President conducts as chief of state are those that take place in the United States, where the American people are watching first hand. An example is when 52 Americans held hostage in Iran for 444 days were at last released to fly home on January 20, 1981—Inauguration Day. They arrived in the capital two days later. There, they boarded buses for a motorcade along Pennsylvania Avenue to the White House. On the South Lawn, fully 6,000 people waited, among them members of Congress and the Cabinet, presidential staff, detachments representing the armed forces, the first lady, and the new chief of state—Ronald Reagan.

Yellow ribbons, which Americans had made symbols of hope and hostage release, festooned the area, and Nancy Reagan wore a yellow dress. There were also 53 American flags, one for each of the 52 former hostages and one for a hostage who had been released early because of illness and flown home the previous July.

Standing at a podium on the South Porch, President Reagan said: "Welcome home. You are home and you are welcome," the greetings of the entire nation. Later, as a token of this greeting, the former hostages each received a rosewood box. Along with the American Flag, engraved in the box was the chief of state's signature.

Chief Executive

The job of President is "no bed of roses," as President Abraham Lincoln said long ago. Harry Truman echoed this sentiment, saying "You can't be thin skinned in the presidency. You have to make a decision and always hope you are right."

One of the hardest roles the President assumes is that of chief executive, which is filled with decision making. When the writers of the Constitution placed the "executive power" in the hands of the President and charged that office to "take care that the laws be faithfully executed," they left the matter dangling.

Two schools of thought about that power developed. One held that the executive function was limited to the powers the Constitution listed, plus whatever others Congress might grant. The other point of view held that the words of the Constitution conferred blanket authority to supervise departments and agencies and to run the government generally. The issue has never been resolved except on a case-to-case basis.

Simply stated, the President as chief executive enforces acts of Congress, judgments of federal courts, and treaties. Some people think of *law enforcement* simply as "crime prevention." However, everything from setting up a Congressionally directed system to distribute food stamps to carrying out court orders setting air pollution standards is within the chief executive's domain.

Also in this role, the Constitution gives the President power "to grant reprieves and pardons for offenses against the United States except in cases of impeachment." President Ford made headlines twice in eight days in exercising this prerogative as chief executive.

On Sept. 8, 1974, a little less than a month after President Richard Nixon had resigned from office in connection with the Watergate scandal, Ford, his successor, pardoned him for all federal crimes Nixon might have committed as President. Ford said in granting the pardon that he did so to end divisions within the nation and to "heal the wounds that had festered too long."

Eight days later, Ford announced the Amnesty Program, offering amnesty to draft dodgers of the Vietnam War period. About 22,000 of the approximately 106,000 eligible persons applied for amnesty under the program.

As chief executive, the President has emergency powers. For example, the Taft-Hartley Act authorizes the President to take emergency measures when a labor-management conflict threatens the "national health or safety."

The chief executive nominates members of the Cabinet, justices of the Supreme Court, ambassadors, and other high officials. These nominations must be approved by a majority vote of the Senate. The President can fill thousands of lesser offices without Senate approval.

Presidential appointments can be for existing jobs or newly created offices. The President's role as federal "employer"—even when Senate approval is not involved—has a number of restrictions, however.

The President, for example, appoints members of the Federal Trade Commission (FTC) to 7-year terms. This agency is independent. A Supreme Court decision in the 1930's held that the President could not remove a member of the FTC except for inefficiency, neglect of duty, or official misconduct—none of which was at issue in the case for which the Supreme Court was rendering this decision. The court ruled, in essence, that the FTC was not a "purely executive" agency. So, the President was restricted in dismissing its members.

There are independent "watchdog" agencies under Congressional control that influence the executive branch. The Government Accountability Office for example, examines the finances of government departments and reports its findings to Congress.

As chief executive, the President shapes and determines policy, coordinates and reorga-

Kennedy meets with leaders of the March on Washington in 1963.
Martin Luther King, Jr., is third from the left.

nizes agencies, and issues executive orders. These orders are issued solely by the President under authority given by the Constitution or under statutes enacted by Congress. For example, the President may issue an executive order to establish an agency. These the chief executive can also reorganize or abolish, also by executive order.

The Reagan Administration, as part of its effort to cut federal spending, proposed dismantling two Cabinet-level departments, the Department of Energy and the Department of Education. Heated Congressional debate followed; plans to dismantle the agencies were eventually dropped. Cabinet-level departments may be eliminated only through an act of Congress, by which they are created.

No one can force a chief executive to fill any office created by Congress. Although positions are usually determined quickly, Lyndon Johnson waited three years before staffing the Administrative Conference of the United States.

The President can sometimes, without confirmation, fill positions requiring Senate approval. These are called interim appointments. But the Senate must be in a recess that excludes holidays or temporary adjournments. President Eisenhower chose Chief Justice Earl Warren for the Supreme Court during a recess. However, in order for Warren to remain in office past the end of the next session, Senate approval was eventually needed.

Although ultimately responsible for all aspects of the federal government, no President can hope to supervise personally the myriad of departments, bureaus, and agencies that are under executive control. Including members of the armed forces, the executive branch employs more than 4 million persons in Washington, D.C., and around the country and the world.

Career civil servants directly supervise the parts of the U.S. government's enormous bureaucracy. Many of them work under the general supervision of Cabinet officers and deputy and assistant secretaries. Civil servants are protected by law from removal on political grounds, and the removal process in most cases can be lengthy.

While Presidents and secretaries of departments come and go, the bureaucracy persists to carry on the day-to-day details of law enforcement and other governmental functions. It is the "permanent government." Some Presidents, like Reagan, have successfully trimmed the size of the bureaucracy, but seldom its power. The bureaucracy remains a vital part of government and a challenging component for the chief executive to control.

Foreign Policy Director

The President, as chief executive, appoints ambassadors and ministers to foreign nations. The President works with them, stateside personnel, and the Congress in the role of foreign policy director for the nation.

In war and in peace, the President has the primary responsibility for directing the nation's foreign affairs even though the President shares the making of foreign policy with Congress. The President's capacity for speed, continuity, secrecy, and flexibility of method are qualities of utmost importance in this area of responsibility.

As foreign policy director, the President makes treaties subject to Senate approval. The President's style is crucial—in part because it sets the tone for international communications. At home, the President must further drum up support for treaties and other foreign policies among political leaders and the public.

The foreign policy director of the United States cannot be everywhere at once. The President often relies on envoys to go to foreign heads of state with American proposals. An envoy's power and position in the government varies.

The practice of using envoys began with President Washington, when he sent Gouverneur Morris as executive agent to England. Under Richard Nixon, Secretary of State Henry Kissinger negotiated exceedingly sensitive international issues.

Though the secretary of state is the President's chief adviser and assistant in foreign relations, Woodrow Wilson and Franklin Roosevelt acted largely as their own secretaries of state, doing much of their own diplomatic negotiating. These Presidents relied heavily on personal assistants. On the other hand, John Foster Dulles, under Eisenhower; Henry Kissinger, under Nixon and Ford; Condoleezza Rice, under George W. Bush; and Hillary Rodham Clinton, under Obama, were strong secretaries of state.

As part of the powers of foreign policy director, the President does much more than make treaties and appoint key personnel for foreign negotiations. The President takes part in international conferences and receives the diplomatic representatives of other nations. The President also proposes legislation dealing with foreign aid and other foreign policy-related issues.

Most Presidents have faced at least a few dilemmas in the field of foreign affairs during their time in office. Some Presidents were more successful than others at solving them. Presidential success with treaty making, for example, often hinges on keeping influential senators informed and encouraged during the process of negotiations, especially where sensitive issues are involved.

At the Versailles Peace Conference in France in 1919, Woodrow Wilson spoke for America largely alone. This was a mistake, for there was strong feeling among Republican senators against Wilson's proposal for a League of Nations in which the United States would participate. Involving key senators in the conference would have been wise. The Senate refused to approve the treaty that included the League of Nations.

Perhaps drawing a lesson from that, Franklin D. Roosevelt cultivated both Republican and Democratic senators to win support for American involvement in the United Nations charter in 1945. Later, John F. Kennedy worked closely with Republican senators in developing a 1963 treaty banning nuclear testing in the atmosphere.

Constitutionally, the House of Representatives does not have a hand in treaty making or other aspects of foreign policy. Yet the House can play a role because it holds the nation's purse strings. In many cases, money must be appropriated to carry out a treaty, and it is the House that must approve the appropriation.

Congress has at times passed laws granting itself important powers concerning certain aspects of foreign policy. For example, if Congress wishes to block the sale of military equipment to a foreign nation, an adverse vote by either chamber can block it. In 1981, when President Reagan proposed selling electronic surveillance planes to Saudi Arabia, numerous members of Congress opposed this sale on grounds that Arab possession of the planes might prove detrimental to Israel. Only intense lobbying by the Reagan Administration prevented an adverse vote. The one-house veto was ruled unconstitutional by the Supreme Court in 1983.

The President as foreign policy director may make executive agreements with other nations. These do not have to be approved by the Senate, and most have the force of law. In some cases, laws specify this means to achieve certain goals. In others, Presidents have made executive agreements on their own. An example is one Franklin Roosevelt made with Britain in 1940. F.D.R. agreed to turn over 50 aged destroyers to the British to help them in their war effort against Germany. In exchange, America gained 99-year leases to use bases on British-held territories in the Caribbean.

Personal diplomacy has been part of the presidential style in conducting foreign relations since Woodrow Wilson's time. But few Presidents have had as great an impact on

American foreign policy or turned it around so quickly as did Richard Nixon in China in 1972.

The Nixon Administration had been making efforts to warm relations with the People's Republic of China after 22 years of hostilities. The nation was unaware of how much progress had been made.

On July 15, 1971, Nixon announced on radio that the People's Republic had invited him to China. The President said he had "accepted the invitation with pleasure." The nation was stunned.

Upon his return to Washington, Nixon reported that the trip had been "the week that changed the world." A new era of American foreign relations had dawned. After this piece of personal presidential diplomacy, the United States recognized the People's Republic, ambassadors and other embassy personnel

President George W. Bush meets with members of his Cabinet, including Secretary of State Colin Powell (left) and Secretary of Defense Donald Rumsfeld, in the early days of Bush's administration in 2001.

were exchanged, and trade between China and the United States reopened.

Commander in Chief

The unwieldy federal government offers numerous points of frustration for any President. Yet the President does possess the power to act swiftly—and decisively, too—especially in situations considered extraordinary. War is one of those situations, and the President conducts it as commander in chief of the United States.

The Constitution gives Congress the sole power to declare war. But it names the President head of the armed forces. The people look to the President, a civilian, to keep the nation's defenses strong.

Lincoln ran the Civil War singlehandedly for nearly three months before Congress convened a special session on July 4, 1861. He used his commander in chief powers to their fullest and to some extent unconstitutionally. Lincoln increased the size of the army and navy, designed strategy against the South, suspended habeas corpus, and jailed Southern sympathizers. "As commander in chief of the army and navy," Lincoln said, "in time of war I suppose I have a right to take any measure which may best subdue the enemy."

Harry S. Truman would express much the same sentiment during the Korean War, but his problem was to subdue his general in one of the most powerful tests of will between the presidency and the U.S. military.

General Douglas MacArthur was a hero of the Pacific during World War II—a trusted, politically powerful, even idolized American. Truman did not share that pedestal. But MacArthur was his choice to lead the American troops in Korea in 1950. The same year, MacArthur became overall commander of forces when the conflict officially became a United Nations war.

As MacArthur drove North Korean forces from South Korea, he pursued them northward toward the Chinese border. This alarmed China, which entered the war.

Fearing the possibility of Soviet intervention and the outbreak of a third world war, Truman wished to confine the conflict to Korea. MacArthur did not. He wanted to take it to China proper. It seemed that the general also wished to pursue other strategies contrary to administration policy.

MacArthur issued numerous statements critical of Truman's conduct of the war. The popular general held quite an audience. Truman faced a tough situation. He was under fire for what critics called his "no-win" policy in Korea. But expanding the war made America's European allies nervous, for they, too, dreaded the prospect of another worldwide conflict. Truman fired MacArthur on April 11, 1951, and replaced him with General Matthew Ridgway.

Truman's action stirred up great criticism and condemnation. But, from Truman's point of view, civilian control of the military was at stake. Reaching his decision, he wrote to a friend, "I could do nothing else and still be President of the United States."

As commander in chief, the President decides disputes among the branches of the armed forces—the air force, army, and navy, which includes the marine corps. The coast guard is in the Department of the Navy in war and the Department of Transportation in peace.

War need not be declared for the President to send forces into combat. American intervention in Korea began as a "police action." And President Lyndon Johnson ordered the first U.S. ground troops to South Vietnam in 1965 to protect American bases there while the war between North and South Vietnam heightened. As South Vietnam faltered, Johnson committed U.S. forces more deeply.

The role of commander in chief has become especially sensitive since the advent of nuclear weapons. The armed forces may not use these weapons without presidential approval. By law, only the President can order the use of nuclear weapons of any kind. This makes the task of commander in chief more awesome than it has ever been.

In October 1962, when the United States learned that the Soviet Union had established missiles on Cuba capable of striking U.S. cities, President John F. Kennedy ordered the U.S. Navy to blockade the island nation. Navy vessels were to turn back all ships delivering Soviet missiles to Cuba. Kennedy also called some 14,000 air force reservists to active duty.

The world stood on the brink of war for a week. Kennedy ordered nuclear weapons to be readied. The Soviets finally backed down and removed their missiles. The crisis was over.

The President may assume the role of commander in chief in any situation that might lead to armed conflict. An example not involving nuclear weapons occurred during the Administration of Gerald Ford.

In 1975, Cambodian Communist forces seized the American merchant ship *Mayagüez* in the Gulf of Siam. Ford determined to rescue the vessel and crew immediately using as much force as necessary. Units of marines and naval ships were ordered to the area and help was requested of Cambodia's ally, the People's Republic of China. Within two days, the ship and its crew were released.

In late 2001, George W. Bush authorized the invasion of Afghanistan in response to the terrorist attacks of September 11, 2001, on the World Trade Center in New York City, the Pentagon near Washington, D.C., and the commercial airliner in Pennsylvania. The U.S. accused Afghanistan of harboring and aiding the terrorists who had acted on September 11.

The Iraq War was launched in 2003 with an invasion of Iraq authorized by Bush to remove then-president Saddam Hussein. The rationale for the war—to find and destroy Hussein's weapons of mass destruction—ultimately proved embarrassing to the administration as no weapons were ever found. The U.S. military remained mired in Iraq throughout Bush's term in office.

In April 2011, Barack Obama approved an operation to kill Osama bin Laden, the leader of the terrorist group that attacked the United States on September 11, 2001. In May 2011, a team of Navy SEALs shot and killed bin Laden in his compound in Pakistan.

The President also assumes the commander-in-chief role to deal with domestic disturbances and to enforce laws. As a rule, governors are responsible for maintaining order and law enforcement with states, calling out state militia if necessary. At times, however, Presidents have stepped in with federal troops, not always on request.

Federal force came into play on numerous occasions during efforts to carry out the Supreme Court desegregation orders in the 1950's and 1960's. President Kennedy handled several of these situations. He relied mainly on federal marshals to enforce desegregation rulings, but during violence at the University of Mississippi at Oxford, Kennedy federalized units of the state national guard.

The action occurred when James Meredith was attempting to enroll as the first black

student at the university. His efforts had been frustrated during the entire month of September 1962. Federal marshals were at the university to maintain order.

On Sept. 30, 1962, 2,500 persons, some armed, attacked the marshals with pieces of pipe, jagged chunks of concrete, rocks, and bottles. Shots were fired. A newspaper reporter and a citizen of Oxford were killed.

Thirty-five marshals, fighting back only with tear gas, suffered gunshot wounds, and more than 150 others were injured. Several buildings and vehicles were burned.

Kennedy sent in the national guard. Two hundred were injured in quelling the riot. By dawn the mob had dispersed. Around 200 persons had been arrested, 24 of them students. Meredith registered that morning.

Kennedy had fulfilled his role as commander in chief. In speaking of the incident and of his critics, his thoughts echoed those of two of his predecessors when he said, "I don't really know what other role they would expect the President of the United States to play."

Do You Know?

1. Why is the U.S. President's role unique among leading nations?
2. How many employees does the President have?
3. What is the presidential "hot line"?
4. To what do presidential pardon powers extend?
5. What President is said to have introduced the "spoils system"?
6. Besides the President and Vice-President, how many other high officials of the executive branch are elected?
7. What President started live televised news conferences?
8. How often does the President receive briefings on security matters from the director of the Central Intelligence Agency (CIA)?
9. How much time is allowed for most visits to the President in the White House?

Answers: (1) It combines the roles of chief of state and chief executive; (2) over 4 million; (3) a communications system available to Presidents in case of national emergency; (4) to offenses against the United States, except in case of impeachment; (5) Jackson; (6) None; the President appoints most of them; (7) Kennedy; (8) daily; (9) usually 15 minutes.

Legislative Leader

Almost all Presidents have taken some active role in influencing legislation, or lawmaking. The President has powerful tools—like the veto—with which to influence Congress. Presidential vetoes are seldom overridden, and the threat of one often stops Congress from acting on one of its own proposals.

But no President can enact a law alone. Congress makes the laws. The President proposes programs that require legislation. The Congress can be a help or a hindrance to presidentially sponsored programs.

Whether the President's political party controls Congress does not ensure an easy ride for a legislative program. Members of Congress have constituencies—voters—to which they are responsible. Members of Congress are also sometimes philosophically opposed to programs a President may support. This is true of those who are in the President's party and those who are not.

The President has several methods of gaining Congressional support for programs. One is to invite members to the White House for conversation or consultation. Another is to invite them to luncheons, briefings by executive staff members, or to other gatherings— with cameras often present. The President may also use friendly letters and telephone calls to persuade members of Congress to give their support.

In addition, a President may offer a senator or representative support for a favorite bill in exchange for a needed vote on some presidentially sponsored legislation. A President might also offer to extend—or threaten to cut off—money for a dam or some other public work important to the senator or representative.

Finally, a President can appeal to the people by means of press conferences and radio and television broadcasts, or in person, hoping that the voters will exert pressure on Congress. Ronald Reagan successfully used this approach, among others, for budget and tax programs in 1981.

During his 1980 campaign, Republican Reagan had promised, among other things, to lower both government spending and taxes. The final budget the ousted Carter Administration had offered called for an expenditure of $739.3 billion in fiscal year 1982, beginning Oct. 1, 1981. Reagan backed a plan to reduce that by

more than $50 billion. At the same time he proposed a three-year income tax cut of 30 per cent overall. A federal deficit of some $31 billion would remain, but this stood against the $54.9 billion the Carter budget had projected. Reagan's long-term goal was a balanced budget for fiscal 1984.

President Reagan at the same time wanted to increase the defense allotment to nearly $200 billion. This meant that many of the cuts would come in controversial areas like education, welfare, energy, Medicare, and food stamps.

The Democrats in Congress responded with their own proposals for reducing spending and taxes, but not on the scale Reagan proposed. Democrats held the House. Republicans controlled the Senate, but their automatic support could not be counted upon.

President Reagan enjoyed much personal popularity the spring after his election, and this helped his cause. He also proved a persistent and successful lobbyist among members of Congress. He invited numerous Republican members to the White House for personal talks. He then had 60 Democrats there in groups of five to eight for about an hour each.

At the same time, presidential aides stirred up grass-roots support to put the pressure on Congress. Friendly members of Congress and Vice-President George H. W. Bush journeyed to various states to speak on the budget and tax plans. Aides organized letter-writing campaigns aimed at Congress.

Reagan proved willing to compromise here and there on the budget. But he did not deviate from his principle of a sizable budget reduction.

Victory for the proposed budget cuts came in the Senate in May, then in the House. The story of the tax reduction bill went much the same. The President did not get all he had wanted. But Reagan had proved highly adept in handling the role of legislative leader.

President Reagan continued to be an effective legislative leader in his second term. He successfully lobbied on behalf of his plan for aid to the rebels in Nicaragua. It was not easy to get Congress to approve the plan.

In February 1986, President Reagan asked Congress to approve $100 million to provide military and nonmilitary aid to the rebels in Nicaragua. Congress had stopped aid to the rebels in 1984, and in 1985 approved

*Nixon as foreign policy director meets with Soviet leader Leonid I.
Brezhnev in Washington, D.C. Nixon visited the U.S.S.R. in May 1972.*

only $27 million for nonmilitary aid, such as food and medical supplies.

President Reagan lobbied members of Congress. He addressed citizens' groups, trying to get their support for his plan. The President once again took his case to the American people in a televised address to the nation. He asked that they contact their Congressmen and show their support for his aid package. Finally, sensing defeat, President Reagan agreed to a compromise aid package. But still the bill was defeated in the House.

Reagan then put his hopes on the Senate. Another intense lobbying campaign began. The Senate approved the bill but now it had to return to the House for their approval.

The President's grass-roots support organization conducted a last-minute media campaign. They used radio ads, direct mail, and telephone campaigns in an effort to gain support for the aid package.

President Reagan also got in some last-minute lobbying. He addressed the House by television and made personal phone calls to those members who were thought to be un-decided on the issue. This time the House approved the bill. President Reagan's personal lobbying efforts were credited with swaying critical votes.

The President exercises legislative leadership perhaps most effectively in the role of political leader—the head of a political party. Once elected, the President becomes, by definition, the party leader.

Vice-President Joe Biden represents President Obama in his role as commander in chief as he greets U.S. troops serving in Baghdad, Iraq, in 2011.

Political Leader

A privilege that goes with this role is selecting the party's national committee chairperson. The committee then formally elects that officer. Most Presidents have had enough control of their party to ensure their own renomination or to hand-pick their successors.

In maintaining party leadership, a President must guide numerous points of view within the party, many of which enjoy solid constituent support. The power of patronage is one of the strongest devices the President has to control these views.

Patronage is the power to make appointments to federal jobs. It can include the allocation of federal funds to favored parts of the country, too.

Over the years, patronage has been a means of imposing presidential party discipline. At one time, a great array of federal jobs, even clerk positions, lay open to presidential appointment. Though none did, each new administration was free practically to make a clean sweep of the bureaucracy to make way for employment of the party faithful.

New Presidents were set upon by office seekers, the qualifications of many amounting mainly to having helped get out the vote at election time. The supply of applicants usually far outdistanced the number of jobs to be filled. "It is not the [Civil War] that is killing me," said a weary Abraham Lincoln, his administration barely begun, "but the Pepperton Post Office."

In 1881, a disappointed jobseeker assassinated President James Garfield. His successor, Chester A. Arthur, pushed the Pendleton Act through Congress. It established the Civil

Service Commission—now called the Office of Personnel Management—and merit as the primary qualification for numerous regular civil service appointments. Over the years, positions on the merit list have grown. But there are still thousands of government jobs subject to patronage. Though not so mighty as before, it is still a powerful weapon.

The patronage privilege has its disadvantages, however. It occupies a substantial amount of the President's time. And it can undermine the President's popularity among party members. As President Taft ruefully remarked, one appointment he made produced him "nine enemies and one ingrate."

Presidential power to influence the allocation of federal funds is also still a potent instrument. According to one story, President Lyndon Johnson needled Democratic Senator Frank Church with it.

Church opposed Johnson's Vietnam policy. And, as the story goes, when Johnson criticized him for that, Church responded that he had done no more than agree with newspaper columnist Walter Lippmann. "Well, Frank," Johnson is said to have replied, "the next time you need money to build a dam in your state, you'd better go to Mr. Lippmann."

Popular Leader

Presidents have a unique claim to the nation's attention. As popular leaders, they use their advantageous position to tell the public what they have done or want to do.

Modern Presidents, more and more exposed to the public view, have been greatly concerned over their presidential "image." They have depended heavily on their press secretaries, speechwriters, and other public relations aides, who help them increase their popular appeal and "sell" their policies to the people.

The newspapers, radio, television, and personal appearances by the Presidents all help them get their message across. The press conference began during Woodrow Wilson's administration. But Franklin Roosevelt brought it into its own in the 1940's. He demanded no questions in advance and freely answered reporters in an off-the-cuff manner. And Roosevelt met the press regularly.

John Kennedy was also a master of press conferences. But he went beyond them. He

often invited editors and reporters to special White House meetings for background briefings and casual conversation.

Radio became an instrument of politics in 1920, when for the first time presidential election returns were broadcast. Again, it was F.D.R. who innovated, taking full advantage. He called his broadcasts to the people "fireside chats," and millions listened every time. Here was a President who seemed to enter the home to talk, explain, and report.

Television as the chief means for presidential communication appeared during the Eisenhower years, and since that time press conferences have been televised. Ike usually did not release the filmed conferences without editing. John Kennedy began the practice of appearing live on television screens, and other Presidents have followed his example.

Presidents realize the power of television as a means of shaping public opinion. And, as the nation's popular leaders, they get TV coverage anytime they choose. Everything a President does makes news, and millions of Americans will interrupt their normal activities to watch and listen. Despite television, a

Military aide follows Carter with the "football," full of military secrets.

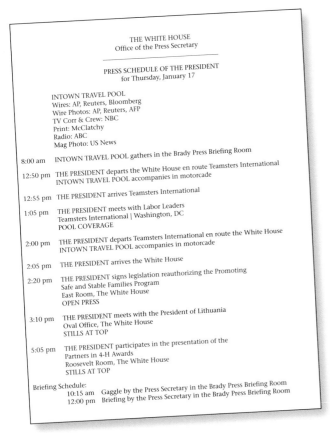

THE WHITE HOUSE
Office of the Press Secretary

PRESS SCHEDULE OF THE PRESIDENT
for Thursday, January 17

INTOWN TRAVEL POOL
Wires: AP, Reuters, Bloomberg
Wire Photos: AP, Reuters, AFP
TV Corr & Crew: NBC
Print: McClatchy
Radio: ABC
Mag Photo: US News

8:00 am   INTOWN TRAVEL POOL gathers in the Brady Press Briefing Room

12:50 pm   THE PRESIDENT departs the White House en route Teamsters International
           INTOWN TRAVEL POOL accompanies in motorcade

12:55 pm   THE PRESIDENT arrives Teamsters International

1:05 pm   THE PRESIDENT meets with Labor Leaders
           Teamsters International | Washington, DC
           POOL COVERAGE

2:00 pm   THE PRESIDENT departs Teamsters International en route the White House
           INTOWN TRAVEL POOL accompanies in motorcade

2:05 pm   THE PRESIDENT arrives the White House

2:20 pm   THE PRESIDENT signs legislation reauthorizing the Promoting
           Safe and Stable Families Program
           East Room, The White House
           OPEN PRESS

3:10 pm   THE PRESIDENT meets with the President of Lithuania
           Oval Office, The White House
           STILLS AT TOP

5:05 pm   THE PRESIDENT participates in the presentation of the
           Partners in 4-H Awards
           Roosevelt Room, The White House
           STILLS AT TOP

Briefing Schedule:
           10:15 am   Gaggle by the Press Secretary in the Brady Press Briefing Room
           12:00 pm   Briefing by the Press Secretary in the Brady Press Briefing Room

*A daily schedule shows the varied responsibilities of
the President.*

personal appearance by the President is still an effective way to shape opinion. Harry Truman showed this in 1948, when he physically took his battered public image to the people via a Pullman car in his whistle-stop campaign for re-election.

Republicans figured that in 1948, most anyone could beat Truman, who had become President when Franklin Roosevelt died in 1945. Problems that had plagued Truman's administration included labor unrest, inflation, the troubled transition from World War II to peacetime, and an uncooperative Congress. Truman had done well in some areas, such as foreign policy. But in April 1948, a Gallup Poll showed that barely a third—36 per cent—of the American people approved his handling of the presidency.

Truman was unpopular with his own party. But the Democrats saw no other candidate in sight for the campaign. They nominated Truman in July 1948, resigned that they had to go with a sure loser. Truman and his advisers decided that he had nothing to lose by going on the attack. And attack he did.

In June and in the months of September and October, Truman rode the rails for reelection.

First Lady Bess and daughter Margaret joined him in the fall on the Pullman car *Ferdinand Magellan*, crisscrossing the country in what he called "the greatest campaign any President ever made." Truman was going to make sure that the people knew where he stood.

The 80th Congress, Democrats and Republicans alike, were Truman's target. As he blasted his views before a crowd at the depot in one small town, someone shouted back, "Give 'em hell, Harry!" That became the catchphrase of the campaign.

The turnouts were phenomenal. But Truman's opponent, Thomas E. Dewey, was confident. The polls had not changed, and the polling stopped in October. It seemed a waste of time. But Truman did not stop. And in November, he won to the astonishment of many.

Harry Truman was a skillful popular leader. He knew how to stir and maintain the people's support. After leaving office, he said:

> The biggest problem facing any President
> is to sell the American people on policy.
> They have to be led forward. . . . That's the
> biggest challenge of every President.

The Vice-President

In February 1982, a furor arose over the possibility of an assassination attempt on the Vice-President's life. What was later believed to have been a rock from a nearby construction site had hit George H. W. Bush's limousine in a capital motorcade. Bush, unharmed and amused, told reporters that in his job, he was not used to that kind of attention. The nation laughed with him when the spot was televised in the news.

The U.S. Constitution gives the Vice-President no official duty other than that of presiding over the U.S. Senate as president of the Senate. The only vice-presidential power is to break a tie vote in that house. For more than 100 years, the absence of political importance of the job caused it to be treated as somewhat of a joke. Some humorously suggested that the Vice-President should be addressed as "Your Superfluous Excellency."

Even today, Vice-Presidents who have assumed office on the death of a President are called "accidental Presidents."

But the prestige of the vice-presidency has gradually increased since the early 1920's, and today the office is as important as the President makes it. Some Presidents have relied on the Vice-President's advice about party policy and political appointments. The Vice-President's participation in Cabinet meetings also depends on the wishes of the President.

The Vice-President's attendance at conferences between the President and Congressional leaders strengthens the Vice-President's influence with the legislative branch. If the President gives the Vice-President important diplomatic missions, the Vice-President can help shape the foreign policy of the United States.

No matter what role the President chooses for the office, the Vice-President is only a heartbeat away from the most powerful elective office in the world. The Vice-President must be ready to become President or acting President at a moment's notice. Nine Vice-Presidents have succeeded to the presidency, eight through death and one through resignation.

The Vice-President has offices in the White House, the Capitol, a U.S. Senate office building, and the Executive Office Building. In 1974, a 33-room mansion on the grounds of Washington's Naval Observatory became the Vice-President's official residence.

The Vice-President makes numerous public appearances. One of the Vice-President's oldest responsibilities is that of ceremonial assistant to the President. In this capacity, the Vice-President greets visiting dignitaries at the air-

port and performs other ceremonial tasks.

In 1984, Geraldine Ferraro became the first woman chosen as a vice-presidential candidate for a major political party. Ferraro and her presidential running mate, former Vice-President Walter Mondale, were defeated by their Republican opponents, President Ronald Reagan and Vice-President George Bush. Previously, Ferraro had served three terms in the United States House of Representatives.

The second woman chosen as a vice-presidential candidate was Alaska Governor Sarah Palin. She ran in 2008 with Republican candidate, Senator John McCain of Arizona.

The Cabinet

The popular definition for "Cabinet" is the heads of the 15 executive-level departments in the federal government. The members are the attorney general and the secretaries of agriculture, commerce, defense, education, energy, health and human services, homeland security, housing and urban development, the interior, labor, state, transportation, the treasury, and veterans affairs. Some Presidents have asked other officials in the executive branch to take part in Cabinet meetings. They are usually held once a week in the Cabinet Room of the White House.

As department heads, Cabinet members are legal officers of the federal government. The

Chief of state Reagan addresses Congress on the state of the national economy in February 1981.

President appoints them with the advice and consent of the Senate and may dismiss them at any time. They are responsible for administering their department and carrying out government policies.

Each Cabinet member receives a yearly salary as the head of an executive department. In 2016, Cabinet members received $205,700. By custom, Cabinet members resign when a new President takes office. This enables the new chief executive to hand-pick the Cabinet for the new administration.

The influence of the Cabinet on presidential decisions changes. Abraham Lincoln's report on one vote in his Cabinet shows how much its members guided him. Lincoln said that the vote was ayes, 1, and nays, all the rest. The ayes had it. Lincoln had voted aye. On the other hand, later, Grant's Cabinet exercised great policy-making influence.

In the 1950's, Dwight Eisenhower looked upon Cabinet officers somewhat like field generals, advising him on policy and primarily responsible for carrying it out. But the scheme seldom worked well.

Because of different and sometimes conflicting interests, the Cabinet does not work as a unified force with the goal of furthering a leader's strategy. Nor does it function like a board of directors, which, after discussion and debate, by a majority vote decides policy. The Cabinet is an unwieldy institution as an advisory body.

In President Kennedy's opinion, Cabinet meetings were useless. "Why should the postmaster," he asked, ". . . listen to a discussion of the problems of Laos?" Kennedy held only six Cabinet meetings during the over two years he was in office, relying on other advisers in making important foreign and domestic policy decisions. But Kennedy did not ignore his Cabinet. He required weekly reports from its members concerning proposals and activities of their departments.

Richard Nixon also seldom called his Cabinet together. In the early 1970's, for example, national economic policy was largely determined by four persons. Of this group, only the secretary of the treasury belonged to the Cabinet. The others were the chief of the Council of Economic Advisers, the director of the Office of Management and Budget, and the head of the Federal Reserve Board. In matters of foreign policy and defense, the National Security Council played a more important part than the Cabinet.

Another reason the President has difficulty using the Cabinet as an advisory body is that the membership may frequently change. President Gerald Ford, during a term of office spanning scarcely two years, had three interior secretaries and two each for commerce and labor.

George W. and Laura Bush, George H. W. and Barbara Bush, and Bill, Hillary, and Chelsea Clinton (front row) pray for the victims of the September 11, 2001, terrorist attack on the United States.

Since the late 1970's, four departments have been added to the Cabinet. Congress created the Department of Energy in 1977 and the Department of Education in 1979—both during the Carter Administration. In 1988, during the Reagan Administration, Congress passed a bill making the Veterans Administration, which administers benefits to veterans of U.S. military service and their dependents, an executive department. The bill renamed the Veterans Administration the Department of Veterans Affairs.

In 2002, the Department of Homeland Security was established after the terrorist attacks of September 11, 2001. The purpose of the department is to coordinate a national strategy to strengthen protections against terrorist threats or attacks in the United States.

The Executive Office

The Executive Office assists the President in many duties. Agencies within the office have come and gone as need has required.

In the early 2000's, these agencies included the Office of Management and Budget, responsible for coordinating federal programs and preparing the federal budget for presentation to Congress, and the Council on Environmental Quality, charged with overseeing federal environmental policies and programs. The National Security Council directs national security programs, drawing information from the Central Intelligence Agency and other intelligence groups within the armed forces, and often coordinating activities with the Department of State. The Council of Economic Advisers reports to the President on economic trends and policies.

The Office of Faith-Based and Community Initiatives, later renamed the Office of Faith-based and Neighborhood Partnerships, was started by George W. Bush in 2001. It implements the President's agenda to empower community and faith-based organizations to better confront poverty and social decay.

Presidents today organize their executive function in great part around the agency called the White House Office. They have always worked with a group of aides, but until 1939 there was no formal organization. Presidents drew their assistants and advisers from groups of friends, from universities, or from various government agencies.

Following the report of a commission on government organization, in 1939, Franklin D. Roosevelt submitted a plan for a White House Office. Congress approved, and Roosevelt established a staff of six members.

By the end of World War II, the White House Office staff had grown to 45. Upon Truman's departure in 1953, he left 250 staff members behind. Under Eisenhower the office increased to more than 400 by the end of his second term in 1961. During the Nixon Administration, it grew to 640. With George W. Bush's Administration, however, the staff was back down to about 400 full-time employees. It rose slightly to about 450 under Barack Obama.

The expense of running such a large agency is considerable. The budget appropriated for the White House Office during Barack Obama's term for fiscal year 2017 (Oct. 1, 2016–Sept. 30, 2017) was $55.2 million.

A small group of advisers drawn from long-time associates of the President forms the core of the White House Office. One might be designated chief domestic counselor, another chief foreign affairs counselor. Some Presidents have named one adviser chief of staff. This person acts as a sort of second in command and as a filter for what and who reaches the eyes and ears of the President.

The nation continues to provide for the Presidents' needs once they leave office. In 2016, the basic annual pension for a retired President was $205,700. They also get free mailing privileges, an allowance for clerical help and office space, and a travel allowance.

In recent times, the aura of chief of state has clung to Presidents in retirement. Some have carried with them prestige and sometimes great influence, and their advice and comments are often sought. But restraints also remain.

There are critics who find it in bad taste for former Presidents to accept employment, for example. Regardless of age, they remain in the ranks of the retired. Activities in which they have been asked to participate include campaigning for party nominees in Congressional and presidential elections and making speeches. Former Presidents have also written books and earned royalties from them.

According to a proposal approved by the Senate in 1963, former Presidents are permitted to speak on the Senate floor. But whatever the podium, in retirement the Presidents serve one final role, as America's foremost elder leaders of state.

Destination:
Pennsylvania Avenue

The White House, at 1600 Pennsylvania Avenue, is a destination that many have sought, but only a privileged few have attained: the Presidents of the United States. George Washington—the first president and the only one elected unanimously—never lived there, although he helped choose the site and approve the design. Most of the Presidents who followed him to the White House had to best rivals in a selection system that became increasingly complicated. Only those who succeeded a deceased President and did not run for a second term were exempt from the problems of seeking the presidency.

A good study of modern elections was the campaign of 1960, in which John F. Kennedy squeaked by Richard M. Nixon by a margin of only about 119,000 popular votes. This election was significant in more ways than simply providing the greatest cliffhanger in 76 years.

First, there was a large number of strong candidates, all vying for public support for their opinions on the state of the nation and how it should be run. In addition, there were political issues that had influenced elections off and on in the past, but not in combination, as they did in 1960—religion, regionalism, youth versus age and experience, wealth in politics, the influence of the media, and the power of political strategy.

Before Conventions

Matters were simpler in the first years of the presidency. There were no political parties, caucuses, conventions, campaign funds, public opinion polls, primaries, or nationwide popular votes then. Transportation—by carriage or horseback—was slow, and communication was by word of mouth, an unreliable postal system, or publications that were unavailable to most people and unintelligible to many. There were no radio and television for a candidate to use in a campaign. There were, in fact, no campaigns. The present system of selecting the President has developed gradually over about 200 years, just as the office of the President has also changed.

National conventions, familiar to Americans today, did not appear as a means of selecting presidential nominees until about 40

Page 46: Four Presidents—past, present, future—at Kennedy's inaugural.

years after the government began operating under the Constitution. Members of the Electoral College, called electors, chose George Washington President in 1789 and again in 1792. As political parties developed, however, the electors became less independent. They still officially elected the President, but the nominees were determined by party caucuses—meetings of party members, most of whom were serving in the Congress or in state legislatures. A caucus of Democratic-Republicans, for example, chose New York Governor George Clinton as their nominee for the vice-presidency in 1792. He lost in the Electoral College to John Adams, the Federalist nominee.

A cartoon depicts the 1824 election race that moved into the House of Representatives when no candidate won an electoral college majority.

Caucuses made up of members of Congress and party leaders usually selected nominees until 1824. The Federalist Party gradually faded, running its last presidential nominee, Rufus King, in 1816. James Monroe secured the Democratic-Republican caucus nomination that year over William H. Crawford of Georgia. Four years later, Monroe was the only candidate in the field.

By 1824, factions within the Democratic-Republican Party had produced five candidates—John Quincy Adams, Andrew Jackson, Speaker of the House Henry Clay of Kentucky, Secretary of War John C. Calhoun of South Carolina, and again Crawford. Most

members of Congress boycotted the caucus that year, and 66 members—nearly three-fourths of them from Georgia, New York, North Carolina, and Virginia—met to nominate Crawford.

As the caucus nominee, Crawford ran under a handicap. Gradually, the right to vote had spread to include all adult white males in most states. In addition, more and more people were participating in party activities. In 1824, electors were chosen by popular vote in 18 out of 24 states. Dissatisfaction with a nominating system that was controlled by a few had grown among voters, and certainly among those who wanted to be

Electoral College

The Electoral College is a group chosen by the voters of each state to elect the President of the United States. This chart shows how the college has voted since 1804, when the present system was adopted. The House of Representatives decided the 1824 election because no one won a majority. In 1872, the electoral votes of Arkansas and Louisiana were disputed and not counted.

Year	Candidate elected	Winner's total	Total vote	Ala.	Alaska	Ariz.	Ark.	Calif.	Colo.	Conn.	Del.	D.C.	Fla.	Ga.	Hawaii	Ida.	Ill.	Ind.	Iowa	Kans.	Ky.	La.	Me.	Md.	Mass.	Mich.	Minn.	Miss.	Mo.	Mont.	Nebr.	Nev.	N.H.
1804	Jefferson	162	176							9	3			6							8		/	19								7
1808	Madison	122	175							9	3			6							7		/	19								7
1812	Madison	128	217							9	4			8							12	3	/	22								8
1816	Monroe	183	217							9	3			8			3				12	3	8	22								8
1820	Monroe	231	232	3						9	4			8			3	3			12	3	9	11	15			2	3				/
1824	J. Q. Adams	84	261							8	1						1					2	9	3	15								8
1828	Jackson	178	261	5						8	3			9			3	5			14	5	/	/	15			3	3				8
1832	Jackson	219	286	7						8	3			11			5	9			15	5	10	/	14			4	4				7
1836	Van Buren	170	294	7			3			8	3			11			5	9			15	5	10	10	14	3		4	4				7
1840	W. Harrison	234	294	7			3			8	3			11			5	9			15	5	10	10	14	3		4	4				7
1844	Polk	170	275	9			3			6	3			10			9	12			12	6	9	8	12	5		6	7				6
1848	Taylor	163	290	9			3			6	3		3	10			9	12	4		12	6	9	8	12	5		6	7				6
1852	Pierce	254	296	9			4	4		6	3		3	10			11	13	4		12	6	8	8	13	6		7	9				5
1856	Buchanan	174	296	9			4	4		6	3		3	10			11	13	4		12	6	8	8	13	6		7	9				5
1860	Lincoln	180	303	9			4	4		6	3		3	10			11	13	4		12	6	8	8	13	6	4	7	9				5
1864	Lincoln	212	233					5		6	3						16	13	8	3	11		7	7	12	8	4		11			2	5
1868	Grant	214	294	8			5	5		6	3		3	9			16	13	8	3	11	7	7	7	12	8	4		11		3	3	5
1872	Grant	286	349	10				6		6	3		4	/			21	15	11	5	/		7	8	13	11	5	8	/		3	3	5
1876	Hayes	185	369	10			6	6	3	6	3		4	11			21	15	11	5	12	8	7	8	13	11	5	8	15		3	3	5
1880	Garfield	214	369	10			6	/	3	6	3		4	11			21	15	11	5	12	8	7	8	13	11	5	8	15		3	3	5
1884	Cleveland	219	401	10			7	8	3	6	3		4	12			22	15	13	9	13	8	6	8	14	13	7	9	16		5	3	4
1888	B. Harrison	233	401	10			7	8	3	6	3		4	12			22	15	13	9	13	8	6	8	14	13	7	9	16		5	3	4
1892	Cleveland	277	444	11			8	/	4	6	3		4	13		3	24	15	13	10	13	8	6	8	15	/	9	9	17	3	8	3	4
1896	McKinley	271	447	11			8	/	4	6	3		4	13		3	24	15	13	10	/		6	8	15	14	9	9	17	3	8	3	4
1900	McKinley	292	447	11			8	9	4	6	3		4	13		3	24	15	13	10	13	8	6	8	15	14	9	9	17	3	8	3	4
1904	T. Roosevelt	336	476	11			9	10	5	7	3		5	13		3	27	15	13	10	13	9	6	/	16	14	11	10	18	3	8	3	4
1908	Taft	321	483	11			9	10	5	7	3		5	13		3	27	15	13	10	13	9	6	/	16	14	11	10	18	3	8	3	4
1912	Wilson	435	531	12		3	9	/	6	7	3		6	14		4	29	15	13	10	13	10	6	8	18	15	12	10	18	4	8	3	4
1916	Wilson	277	531	12		3	9	13	6	7	3		6	14		4	29	15	13	10	13	10	6	8	18	15	12	10	18	4	8	3	4
1920	Harding	404	531	12		3	9	13	6	7	3		6	14		4	29	15	13	10	13	10	6	8	18	15	12	10	18	4	8	3	4
1924	Coolidge	382	531	12		3	9	13	6	7	3		6	14		4	29	15	13	10	13	10	6	8	18	15	12	10	18	4	8	3	4
1928	Hoover	444	531	12		3	9	13	6	7	3		6	14		4	29	15	13	10	13	10	6	8	18	15	12	10	18	4	8	3	4
1932	F. Roosevelt	472	531	11		3	9	22	6	8	3		7	12		4	29	14	11	9	11	10	5	8	17	19	11	9	15	4	7	3	4
1936	F. Roosevelt	523	531	11		3	9	22	6	8	3		7	12		4	29	14	11	9	11	10	5	8	17	19	11	9	15	4	7	3	4
1940	F. Roosevelt	449	531	11		3	9	22	6	8	3		7	12		4	29	14	11	9	11	10	5	8	17	19	11	9	15	4	7	3	4
1944	F. Roosevelt	432	531	11		4	9	25	6	8	3		8	12		4	28	13	10	8	11	10	5	8	16	19	11	9	15	4	6	3	4
1948	Truman	303	531	11		4	9	25	6	8	3		8	12		4	28	13	10	8	11	10	5	8	16	19	11	9	15	4	6	3	4
1952	Eisenhower	442	531	11		4	8	32	6	8	3		10	12		4	27	13	10	8	10	10	5	9	16	20	11	8	13	4	6	3	4
1956	Eisenhower	457	531	/		4	8	32	6	8	3		10	12		4	27	13	10	8	10	10	5	9	16	20	11	8	13	4	6	3	4
1960	Kennedy	303	537	/	3	4	8	32	6	8	3		10	12	3	4	27	13	10	8	10	10	5	9	16	20	11	8	13	4	6	3	4
1964	L. Johnson	486	538	10	3	5	6	40	6	8	3	3	14	12	4	4	26	13	9	7	9	10	4	10	14	21	10	7	12	4	5	3	4
1968	Nixon	301	538	10	3	5	6	40	6	8	3	3	14	12	4	4	26	13	9	7	9	10	4	10	14	21	10	7	12	4	5	3	4
1972	Nixon	520	538	9	3	6	6	45	7	8	3	3	17	12	4	4	26	13	8	7	9	10	4	10	14	21	10	7	12	4	5	3	4
1976	Carter	297	538	9	3	6	6	45	7	8	3	3	17	12	4	4	26	13	8	7	9	10	4	10	14	21	10	7	12	4	5	3	4
1980	Reagan	489	538	9	3	6	6	45	7	8	3	3	17	12	4	4	26	13	8	7	9	10	4	10	14	21	10	7	12	4	5	3	4
1984	Reagan	525	538	9	3	7	6	47	8	8	3	3	21	12	4	4	24	12	8	7	9	10	4	10	13	20	10	7	11	4	5	4	4
1988	G. H. W. Bush	426	538	9	3	7	6	47	8	8	3	3	21	12	4	4	24	12	8	7	9	10	4	10	13	20	10	7	11	4	5	4	4
1992	Clinton	370	538	9	3	8	6	54	8	8	3	3	25	13	4	4	22	12	7	6	8	9	4	10	12	18	10	7	11	3	5	4	4
1996	Clinton	379	538	9	3	8	6	54	8	8	3	3	25	13	4	4	22	12	7	6	8	9	4	10	12	18	10	7	11	3	5	4	4
2000	G. W. Bush	271	538	9	3	8	6	54	8	8	3	/	25	13	4	4	22	12	7	6	8	9	4	10	12	18	10	7	11	3	5	4	4
2004	G. W. Bush	286	538	9	3	10	6	55	9	7	3	3	27	15	4	4	21	11	7	6	8	9	4	10	12	17	10	6	11	3	5	5	4
2008	Obama	365	538	9	3	10	6	55	9	7	3	3	27	15	4	4	21	11	7	6	8	9	4	10	12	17	10	6	11	3	/	5	4
2012	Obama	332	538	9	3	11	6	55	9	7	3	3	29	16	4	4	20	11	6	6	8	8	4	10	11	16	10	6	10	3	5	6	4
2016	Trump	306	538	9	3	11	6	55	9	7	3	3	29	16	4	4	20	11	6	6	8	8	/	10	11	16	10	6	10	3	5	6	4

Legend:
- ☐ Democratic
- ☐ Democratic-Republican
- ☐ National Republican
- ☐ Progressive
- ☑ Split vote
- ☐ Republican
- ☐ Federalist
- ☐ Whig
- ☐ Other parties
- ☐ Not voting

N.J.	N.Mex.	N.Y.	N.C.	N.Dak.	Ohio	Okla.	Ore.	Pa.	R.I.	S.C.	S.Dak.	Tenn.	Tex.	Utah	Vt.	Va.	Wash.	W.Va.	Wis.	Wyo.	Year
8		19	14		3			20	4	10		5			6	24					1804
8		/	/		3			20	4	10		5			6	24					1808
8		29	15		7			25	4	11		8			8	25					1812
8		29	15		8			25	4	11		8			8	25					1816
8		29	15		8			24	4	11		7			8	25					1820
		26							4						7						1824
8		/	15		16			28	4	11		11			7	24					1828
8		42	15		21			30	4	11		15			7	23					1832
8		42	15		21			30	4	11		15			7	23					1836
8		42	15		21			30	4	11		15			7	23					1840
7		36	11		23			26	4	9		13			6	17					1844
7		36	11		23			26	4	9		13	4		6	17			4		1848
7		35	10		23			27	4	8		12	4		5	15			5		1852
7		35	10		23			27	4	8		12	4		5	15			5		1856
/		35	10		23		3	27	4	8		12	4		5	15			5		1860
7		33			21		3	26	4						5			5	8		1864
7		33	9		21		3	26	4	6		10			5			5	8		1868
9		35	10		22		3	29	4	7		12	8		5	11		5	10		1872
9		35	10		22		3	29	4	7		12	8		5	11		5	10		1876
9		35	10		22		3	29	4	7		12	8		5	11		5	10		1880
9		36	11		23		3	30	4	9		12	13		4	12		6	11		1884
9		36	11		23		3	30	4	9		12	13		4	12		6	11		1888
10		36	11	/	/		/	32	4	9	4	12	15		4	12	4	6	12	3	1892
10		36	11	3	23		4	32	4	9	4	12	15	3	4	12	4	6	12	3	1896
10		36	11	3	23		4	32	4	9	4	12	15	3	4	12	4	6	12	3	1900
12		39	12	4	23		4	34	4	9	4	12	18	3	4	12	5	7	13	3	1904
12		39	12	4	23	7	4	34	4	9	4	12	18	3	4	12	5	7	13	3	1908
14	3	45	12	5	24	10	5	38	5	9	5	12	20	4	4	12	7	8	13	3	1912
14	3	45	12	5	24	10	5	38	5	9	5	12	20	4	4	12	7	/	13	3	1916
14	3	45	12	5	24	10	5	38	5	9	5	12	20	4	4	12	7	8	13	3	1920
14	3	45	12	5	24	10	5	38	5	9	5	12	20	4	4	12	7	8	13	3	1924
14	3	45	12	5	24	10	5	38	5	9	5	12	20	4	4	12	7	8	13	3	1928
16	3	47	13	4	26	11	5	36	4	8	4	11	23	4	3	11	8	8	12	3	1932
16	3	47	13	4	26	11	5	36	4	8	4	11	23	4	3	11	8	8	12	3	1936
16	3	47	13	4	26	11	5	36	4	8	4	11	23	4	3	11	8	8	12	3	1940
16	4	47	14	4	25	10	6	35	4	8	4	12	23	4	3	11	8	8	12	3	1944
16	4	47	14	4	25	10	6	35	4	8	4	/	23	4	3	11	8	8	12	3	1948
16	4	45	14	4	25	8	6	32	4	8	4	11	24	4	3	12	9	8	12	3	1952
16	4	45	14	4	25	8	6	32	4	8	4	11	24	4	3	12	9	8	12	3	1956
16	4	45	14	4	25	/	6	32	4	8	4	11	24	4	3	12	9	8	12	3	1960
17	4	43	13	4	26	8	6	29	4	8	4	11	25	4	3	12	9	7	12	3	1964
17	4	43	/	4	26	8	6	29	4	8	4	11	25	4	3	12	9	7	12	3	1968
17	4	41	13	3	25	8	6	27	4	8	4	10	26	4	3	/	9	6	11	3	1972
17	4	41	13	3	25	8	6	27	4	8	4	10	26	4	3	12	/	6	11	3	1976
17	4	41	13	3	25	8	6	27	4	8	4	10	26	4	3	12	9	6	11	3	1980
16	5	36	13	3	23	8	7	25	4	8	3	11	29	5	3	12	10	6	11	3	1984
16	5	36	13	3	23	8	7	25	4	8	3	11	29	5	3	12	10	/	11	3	1988
15	5	33	14	3	21	8	7	23	4	8	3	11	32	5	3	13	11	5	11	3	1992
15	5	33	14	3	21	8	7	23	4	8	3	11	32	5	3	13	11	5	11	3	1996
15	5	33	14	3	21	8	7	23	4	8	3	11	32	5	3	13	11	5	11	3	2000
15	5	31	15	3	20	7	7	21	4	8	3	11	34	5	3	13	11	5	10	3	2004
15	5	31	15	3	20	7	7	21	4	8	3	11	34	5	3	13	11	5	10	3	2008
14	5	29	15	3	18	7	7	20	4	9	3	11	38	6	3	13	12	5	10	3	2012
14	5	29	15	3	18	7	7	20	4	9	3	11	38	6	3	13	12	5	10	3	2016

Splits in State Electoral Votes

In most elections, the candidate who wins the highest number of a state's popular votes receives all the state's electoral votes. In some elections, however, Electoral College members from the same state have voted for different candidates. This situation is shown by a slash mark (/) in the table on these two pages. Since 1804, the following splits in state electoral votes have occurred:

Election	State's Total Vote and Split
1804	Maryland 11 (Jefferson 9, Charles C. Pinckney 2)
1808	Maryland 11 (Madison 9, Pinckney 2); New York 19 (Madison 13, George Clinton 6); North Carolina 14 (Madison 11, Pinckney 3)
1812	Maryland 11 (Madison 6, Clinton 5)
1820	New Hampshire 8 (Monroe 7, J. Q. Adams 1)
1828	Maine 9 (J. Q. Adams 8, Jackson 1); Maryland 11 (J. Q. Adams 6, Jackson 5); New York 36 (Jackson 20, J. Q. Adams 16)
1832	Maryland 8 (Henry Clay 5, Jackson 3)
1860	New Jersey 7 (Lincoln 4, Stephen A. Douglas 3)
1872	Georgia 8 (Benjamin G. Brown 6, Charles J. Jenkins 2); Kentucky 12 (Thomas A. Hendricks 8, Brown 4); Missouri 15 (Brown 8, Hendricks 6, David Davis 1)
1880	California 6 (Winfield Scott Hancock 5, Garfield 1)
1892	California 9 (Cleveland 8, B. Harrison 1); Michigan 14 (B. Harrison 9, Cleveland 5); North Dakota 3 (Cleveland 1, B. Harrison 1, James B. Weaver 1); Ohio 23 (B. Harrison 22, Cleveland 1); Oregon 4 (B. Harrison 3, Weaver 1)
1896	California 9 (McKinley 8, William Jennings Bryan 1); Kentucky 13 (McKinley 12, Bryan 1)
1904	Maryland 8 (Alton B. Parker 7, T. Roosevelt 1)
1908	Maryland 8 (Bryan 6, Taft 2)
1912	California 13 (T. Roosevelt 11, Wilson 2)
1916	West Virginia 8 (Charles E. Hughes 7, Wilson 1)
1948	Tennessee 12 (Truman 11, Strom Thurmond 1)
1956	Alabama 11 (Adlai E. Stevenson 10, Walter B. Jones 1)
1960	Alabama 11 (Harry F. Byrd 6, Kennedy 5); Oklahoma 8 (Nixon 7, Byrd 1)
1968	North Carolina 13 (Nixon 12, George C. Wallace 1)
1972	Virginia 12 (Nixon 11, John Hospers 1)
1976	Washington 9 (Ford 8, Reagan 1)
1988	West Virginia 6 (Michael S. Dukakis 5, Lloyd Bentsen 1)
2000	Washington, D.C. 3 (Al Gore 2, abstention 1)
2008	Nebraska 5 (John McCain 4, Barack Obama 1)
2016	Maine 4 (Hillary Clinton 3, Trump 1)

*Unofficial
For official results, see
http://www.archives.gov/federal-register/electoral-college/

The log cabin was a symbol of William H. Harrison's 1840 campaign.

President in 1824. "King Caucus" had become terminally ill.

State legislatures nominated Jackson, Adams, Calhoun, and Clay to oppose Crawford in 1824. Calhoun withdrew, presenting himself as the anticaucus vice-presidential candidate. His ambition was fulfilled, but no nominee received a majority of presidential electoral votes. Consequently, the House of Representatives, following the Constitution, named the winner, electing John Quincy Adams after a heated contest.

Conventions in the states, state legislatures, and mass meetings endorsed John Quincy Adams and Andrew Jackson in 1828. By then the Democratic-Republicans had become National Republicans, and the new Democratic-Republican Party, later called the Democratic Party, had formed around Jackson. He won a majority of electoral votes, sweeping Adams out of office after one term.

Then in 1832, the first third party, the Anti-Masonic, appeared. This group, formed in New York, was to some extent an outgrowth of the democratic fervor of the time. The party focused its attention mainly on opposition to the Masons, a secret fraternal organization whose members at that time came largely from the upper social and economic classes. The

Anti-Masons appealed to the laboring and small farmer classes and also tended to be against slavery and cities.

The First Convention

Anti-Masonism was strongest in New England and the Middle Atlantic States. In 1831, the party became the first to hold a national nominating convention. This occurred in September in Baltimore. The 116 delegates from 13 states nominated William Wirt, former attorney general of Maryland, for the presidency. In 1832, Wirt gained 100,712 votes and carried one state, Vermont. The party also elected Vermont's governor and 53 members of Congress.

But 1832 proved to be high tide for the Anti-Masons. The party soon faded, most of its members moving into the Whig Party, which grew out of the National Republican Party.

The National Republicans held their own convention in Baltimore in 1831, choosing Henry Clay. The next year, the Democrats met in convention to name Andrew Jackson for re-election. Although the Whigs did not meet in 1836, the Democrats had gathered again in Baltimore in 1835, nominating Martin Van Buren, who had been Jackson's Vice-President during his second term. And that Baltimore conclave was a loose affair, judging from this account:

> Twenty-two states and two territories—Michigan and Arkansas—were represented. No delegates were present from Illinois, South Carolina, or Alabama.... A list of those who took part contains 626 names. Of these, 422 came from the states of Maryland, Virginia, New Jersey, and Pennsylvania. Maryland is mentioned first because it contributed 181 members. The Maryland state convention, called to select delegates, was apparently unwilling to deny any of its own members an opportunity to take part, and accordingly resolved that all of them should be delegates. Virginia sent 108, New Jersey 73, and Pennsylvania 60, being two contesting delegations of 30 each. On the other hand, Tennessee sent no delegates; but a citizen of the state who would vote for Van Buren, chancing to be in Baltimore, presented himself, was admitted, and cast the 15 votes allotted to Tennessee.

{}

*Political cartoonists enjoyed lampooning
President Buchanan's small tuft of hair.*

*President Lincoln's lanky figure was
the butt of many political cartoons.*

After 1836, national nominating conventions
became standard with the major political parties.
Over the years, many forms of strategic convention maneuvering developed on the part of candidates, such as planning for and taking advantage of convention deadlocks. The planning of
many of the candidates before the 1960 Democratic convention was filled with just such strategy.

Although President Dwight D. Eisenhower
enjoyed great public support, all was not well
with Republicans as the 1960 elections
approached. The economy was only slowly
pulling out of a recession that began in 1957.
The Soviet Union had launched the world's first
manufactured satellite that year, surprising
Americans and calling into question the Eisenhower Administration's policies regarding
space, missiles, science education, and national
defense. Although Eisenhower had been elected
twice by large majorities, he held himself aloof
from Republican Party matters and contributed
little to maintaining a sound party organization.
Moreover, Democrats had gained control of Congress in 1954. As Democratic prospects bright-
ened, several prominent party members began
measuring their chances of winning the nation's
highest office.

One was Senator Lyndon B. Johnson of
Texas, who since his election to the House in

Campaign Memorabilia

An 1884 campaign poster shows Cleveland and Hendricks against a background of patriotic symbols and admired Presidents.

An 1896 cologne bottle bears the image of Democratic candidate William Jennings Bryan.

"I Like Ike" ties identified supporters of Eisenhower in his 1956 re-election campaign.

A metal serving tray bears images of 1908 Republican candidates Taft and Sherman, with previous GOP leaders.

This flag waved for candidates James K. Polk and George M. Dallas in their 1844 campaign.

Pens and pencils, like this Truman pencil from 1948, have long been popular campaign giveaways.

A Nixon umbrella from the 1960 election; campaign umbrellas were especially popular in campaigns from 1896 to 1904.

*Abraham Lincoln and Stephen Douglas are shown fighting for
the presidency of 1860 in a contemporary American cartoon.*

1937 had become a power in Congress and a
Senate leader in the 1950's. Johnson was a master of the national legislative process. He dominated the Senate, and there was hardly a member of Congress who did not owe him a favor
for getting some piece of legislation passed. A
majority of the members of the Senate named
Johnson their favorite for the presidency.

Convention Strategy

Johnson and those who supported him
were one of the groups basing its strategy on
the likelihood of a convention deadlock over
the nomination. In the event of a stalemate,
they would then rally Congressional support
for his candidacy. At the same time, in the
spring of 1960, Johnson also tried to gain support from state Democratic leaders, although
he was not well known to most of them.

Another who counted on deadlock was
Senator Stuart Symington of Missouri. His

plans for action differed somewhat from
Johnson's, however.

Symington had been elected to the Senate
in 1952 and had won re-election in 1958 by an
overwhelming 66 per cent majority. Previously he had served as secretary of the air force
under President Harry S. Truman, and in the
Senate his major interest had been the nation's
military preparedness. Symington had proved
an able executive. And besides, he had considerable personal appeal. He was handsome
and looked like a President.

Symington was not well-known nation-
ally, but he could count on support from
Truman and other political leaders in Missouri. He and his strategists believed that this
backing of powerful political bosses in that
state could be expanded in case of a deadlock
during the 1960 Democratic convention.

A third Democratic possibility in 1960
was also a senator, Hubert H. Humphrey of
Minnesota. While in his early 30's, Humphrey had won election as mayor of Minne-

apolis in 1945. Elected to the Senate in 1948, Humphrey had gained prominence at the Democratic convention that year for his fight on behalf of a strong civil rights plank in the party platform. When the convention adopted it, Southern Democrats withdrew to nominate their own candidate, Strom Thurmond of South Carolina, who ran for the presidency on the States' Rights, or Dixiecrat ticket.

Humphrey furthered his reputation as a liberal in the Senate. He spoke out on many issues, such as farm supports, labor unions, disarmament, education, civil rights, housing, and welfare. Humphrey had actively sought the vice-presidential nomination in 1956 but had failed.

Even though he had lost the last two presidential elections to Dwight D. Eisenhower, there was still support among Democrats for former Governor Adlai E. Stevenson of Illinois. A refined and witty man, Stevenson sought the high road in politics. While he looked upon politics as a noble calling, he had little stomach for what he considered the grubby details of campaigning and electioneering.

The presidency and its power attracted Stevenson. But while groups formed in several states to promote his nomination in 1960, Stevenson refused to seek the party's nod. He considered it his duty to serve if called upon, but he would not put himself forward. Stevenson held that position until, to his dismay, it became too late to change his mind.

The fourth active candidate for the Democratic nomination was another senator, John F. Kennedy of Massachusetts. Born in 1917, Kennedy was the youngest to enter the field. He came from a large family with considerable wealth. His father, Joseph, had accumulated a fortune on Wall Street and in real estate. The elder Kennedy had also served as ambassador to Great Britain under Franklin D. Roosevelt, and he had strong political connections in Massachusetts and other Eastern states.

After graduating from Harvard University in 1940, John Kennedy served in the navy during World War II. He won election to the House of Representatives in 1946, to the Senate in 1952, and was re-elected six years later.

Like Humphrey, Kennedy had tried for the vice-presidential nomination in 1956. He decided then to try for the presidency four years later, and appeared at Democratic gath-

A 1880 Thomas Nast cartoon helped popularize the Democratic donkey symbol.

erings in all 50 states during the next three years.

Johnson's and Symington's deadlock strategy seemed sound. As 1960 began, there was no Democratic front-runner, the position Vice-President Richard Nixon enjoyed in the Republican Party. In the past, there had been stand-offs in both parties that even allowed little-known, "surprise" candidates—called "dark-horses"—to grab the nomination. It happened for the first time at the Democratic convention in Baltimore in May 1844.

Former President Martin Van Buren was the leading candidate at the start of the convention, closely followed by Lewis Cass of Michigan. On the first seven ballots, no candidate could get enough votes to claim the nomination. But on the third day, Governor Henry Hubbard of New Hampshire nominated James K. Polk, a former member of the House of Representatives and governor from Tennessee. Polk picked up 44 votes on the eighth ballot and won the nomination on the ninth.

Warren G. Harding emerged as the dark-horse candidate at the Republican convention in Chicago in 1920. A lackluster senator from Ohio, Harding relied on guidance from Harry Daugherty, a politician from that state who looked forward to a deadlock that year.

58 The President's World

Although announced as a candidate, Harding aroused no enthusiasm when the convention opened. Delegates split over Governor Frank O. Lowden of Illinois; Major General Leonard Wood, a soldier and colonial administrator; and Senator Hiram Johnson of California. Those three seesawed back and forth during four ballots on the first day of voting.

That evening, Republican leaders got together in a Chicago hotel to discuss a compromise nominee. After several hours, Harding appeared acceptable to most of them.

As balloting resumed the next day, Harding gained steadily. By the ninth ballot he was ahead, and he won on the 10th.

The 1960 Primaries

Humphrey was not well-known among voters in general in 1960, and Kennedy was even less so. Both were bucking strong competition in Johnson ad Symington, and both viewed primary elections as the only way they could build popular support and influence party leaders.

In 1960 there were Democratic presidential primaries in the District of Columbia and 15 states—California, Florida, Illinois, Indiana, Maryland, Massachusetts, Nebraska, New Hampshire, New Jersey, Ohio, Oregon, Pennsylvania, South Dakota, West Virginia, and Wisconsin. Humphrey entered five, Kennedy seven.

Primaries are a fairly recent device for testing candidate appeal. They arose when nominating conventions no longer seemed the most democratic method of choosing nominees. Conventions had fallen under the con-trol of political bosses, who made decisions and then more or less presented them to the convention delegates for endorsement.

Change in the nominating procedure began on the state level, perhaps because of the governor's race in Wisconsin at the turn of the 20th century. Republican Party bosses in Wisconsin had denied Robert M. La Follette a chance at the governorship in 1896 and 1898. In both years, La Follette went into the state Republican convention with considerable delegate support, yet failed to get the nomination. By 1900, La Follette had settled

The elephant as a symbol of the Republican Party made its first appearance in print in this 1874 cartoon by Thomas Nast.

differences with the bosses and he was nominated and elected governor. By that time, he had become convinced, however, that a different means of reflecting popular will in choosing nominees had to be found. He settled on the primary election.

La Follette did not invent the primary. Democrats in Pennsylvania has used it first in the 1840's, and in various parts of the country, the primary was used on a optional basis before 1900. But La Follette made it mandatory on a statewide basis.

Wisconsin enacted a direct primary law in 1903 and the state's voters approved it in a referendum in 1904. Candidates for state offices had to secure a certain number of signatures on nominating petitions in order to get on the ballot. In the primary election, voters would choose the candidates who would appear on the lists in the general election. Later, the primary idea was applied to selecting national convention delegates to choose presidential nominees.

The direct primary did not eliminate state political conventions. Those were still held to handle such party business as writing platforms. But the primary gave citizens a direct hand in selecting nominees for public office.

For most states holding presidential primaries today, each candidate wishing to enter the election lists a slate of delegates from the state promised to support the candidate at the national convention. Party members show their choice for the presidential nomination by voting for the slate of delegates committed to that candidate. There are several variations in this complicated system. One is the presidential preferential primary, where the voters choose delegates to the convention, but the delegates are not bound to support the candidates they represent. And some states' delegates are committed only in part. Some are bound to the primary winner and some may vote as they wish. In addition, some delegates' votes are bound for only the first or second vote.

In 1912, 13 states had some form of presidential primary. Most of them were closed primaries. That is, at the polling place, each voter had to declare a party preference before receiving a ballot, which contained only that party's primary candidates. Wisconsin was one of the few states to hold an open primary. In this form no stated party preference was required, and voters received ballots contain-

Uncle Sam scrutinizes "Little Ben" Harrison, grandson to W. H. Harrison.

ing the names of candidates for all parties. They could "cross over" from one party to another as they chose. In other words, Democrats could vote for Republicans and vice versa.

In the 1920's, primaries did not seem influential. Between 1912 and 1924, their results and convention outcomes on nominees coincided only three out of eight times. And in two of those three cases, incumbent Presidents Woodrow Wilson and Calvin Coolidge were seeking the nomination.

Part of the problem lay in delegate commitment. Delegates from some states were not bound to vote for any particular candidate at the convention. And many delegates were bound only for the first or second ballot. Moreover, some states could send one group of delegates supporting one candidate and another endorsing a second. And, even in 1912, less than one-third of the states held primaries. Conventions or committees chose delegates in the others.

The number of primary states continued to decline. By 1960, it rested at 15 Republican and 16 Democratic.

John F. Kennedy faced the 1960 primaries with two disadvantages. One was his youth. He was only 43 and looked younger. Youth signaled inexperience to many voters, arousing doubt concerning his ability to handle crises. The other disadvantage was Kennedy's religion.

Many influences bear on voters. Party loyalty, family political preferences and habits, ethnic considerations, and social and economic status are among them. Religion is also a consideration. It had long been assumed that a Roman Catholic could not be elected President of the United States. One Catholic, Alfred E. Smith, the Democratic governor of New York, ran in 1928 and lost.

Many observers contended that this religious barrier applied only to the presidency. Innumerable Catholics had been elected to local and state offices. The concern with regard to the presidency seemed to center on relations between church and state. Traditionally, the Catholic church in Europe and Latin America had maintained a close relationship to the national government. In the United States, however, the First Amendment to the Constitution keeps church and state separate, a feature of vital importance to the American political system. The fear existed among many Americans that a Catholic President might be inclined to breach that wall of separation, or at least weaken it. This was the issue Kennedy set out to quiet in 1960.

The first real primary test came in Wisconsin in April, where he met Humphrey head-on. Thirty-one committed Democratic delegates were at stake there. Ten were elected at large, and the primary winner would take all of those. In addition, two delegates would be chosen from each of the state's 10 Congressional districts. The last delegate vote would be shared by two members of the Democratic National Committee from Wisconsin.

Humphrey, representing neighboring Minnesota in the Senate, was well-known among Wisconsinites. Kennedy was a stranger. But Humphrey had relatively few people working for him full-time. He relied on many who could come over from Minnesota. Kennedy could call in brothers and sisters and other relatives, as well as friends, all of whom could work full-time. In addition, the Kennedy forces were able to marshal many volunteers to address envelopes, make phone calls, and distribute campaign literature.

The Kennedy forces blanketed Wisconsin. By primary day the name *Kennedy* was far from unknown there.

During William McKinley's successful 1896 presidential campaign, his campaign buttons promoted the continuation of high protective tariffs. McKinley's opponent, Grover Cleveland, favored attempts to lower the tariff.

The 1900 McKinley-Roosevelt team offered jobs and a "Full Dinner bucket.

Yet results were not completely satisfactory to Kennedy and his advisers. He carried six of the 10 Congressional districts, but four of the six held large Catholic populations. No one could tell how many people had voted along religious lines. Nor did anyone know how many Republicans who were Catholic had cast ballots for Kennedy in Wisconsin, where crossovers were permitted.

Kennedy and Humphrey then geared up for another round in West Virginia. Only about 5 per cent of the people there were Catholic. The Kennedy thrust in the Mountain State was even greater, deeper, and more determined than in Wisconsin. Campaign leaders organized thousands of volunteers to distribute literature door to door, address and mail other material, and conduct telephone campaigns.

Now Kennedy forced the religion issue. Over and over, he made it clear that he stood firmly for the separation of church and state. He declared that religious belief and allegiance would in no way influence his policies should he win the presidency. It appeared that Kennedy persuaded a good many West Virginians. He gradually overcame an early Humphrey opinion poll lead to beat Humphrey by over 84,000 votes.

Humphrey dropped out of the race after West Virginia. Kennedy went on to gain primary votes in eight other states, in some instances as a write-in candidate.

Kennedy's success in Wisconsin and West Virginia helped ease the task of gathering delegates in nonprimary states. As a consequence of the primaries and pledges in other states, by the end of June 1960, Kennedy commanded about 550 votes, and he picked up another 50 before the Democratic convention opened in Los Angeles in July. He needed 761, a majority of the delegates.

The convention itself would be another battleground. Johnson and Symington possessed delegate strength, and there was still support for Stevenson. Each camp would try to pry delegates from the others before the first ballot.

Meanwhile, although he felt confident of Republican Party support, Richard Nixon also placed his name on primary ballots in nine states and was a write-in candidate in two others. Altogether, Nixon gathered nearly 5 million primary votes. His only troublesome rival was Governor Nelson. A. Rockefeller of New York. Any real threat from him had paled by the time the Republican convention convened, however.

Convention Structure

More delegates to national conventions are chosen today by primary elections than ever before. State party conventions or party committees also still name others. The size of a state's delegation reflects its population in proportion to the other states.

The party's national committee chooses the city in which the convention will be held and organizes the convention. That group also appoints members of committees such as rules, credentials, and resolutions. The resolutions committee, with the aid of subcommittees, writes the party platform. It contains the policies the party stands for, which might be turned into legislation or government policy if the party nominee wins.

In order of occurrence, the major events at a convention are: the keynote address, in which a prominent party member presents policies and goals; reading and adopting the platform; nominations and speeches supporting the various nominees; voting for the presidential nominee by states; selecting a vice-presidential nominee; and the presidential nominee's acceptance speech.

The convention schedule and politicking for the presidential candidates proceed together.

Candidates often appear at state delegate caucuses seeking votes. Caucuses are also held to
decide which candidate will get support from
delegates not already committed beyond the
first or second ballot. The quest for support
continues among delegates on the convention
floor.

Few conventions are without their demonstrations—noisy, boisterous displays of support for candidates, during which delegates
wave banners, clap, cheer, and frequently
march around the convention floor. Demonstrations often follow the placing of a name in
nomination.

In the past, conventions often ran behind
schedule, largely because of prolonged demonstrations. Now that conventions are televised, there is a greater tendency to hold to a
schedule and more closely control demonstrations. And because of television, most important official business is conducted at night to
take advantage of a maximum number of
viewers throughout the country.

According to writer H. L. Mencken, who
observed many political gatherings:

A national convention is as fascinating
as a revival or a hanging. It is vulgar,
ugly, stupid, and tedious, to be sure,
and yet there suddenly comes a show
so gaudy and hilarious, so melodra-
matic and obscene, so unimaginably
exhilarating and preposterous that one
lives a gorgeous year in a hour.

Yet, some conventions have been tedious. In
1924, for example, the Democrats ran through
102 ballots in New York City before nominating John W. Davis. Others have generated
excitement. In 1896 in Chicago, during debate
on the party platform, William Jennings Bryan
electrified the convention with his "Cross of
Gold" speech advocating the free coinage of
silver. He swept the Democratic nomination.

There have also been surprises. Wendell L.
Willkie, a power company executive and former Democrat, won the Republican nomination in 1940 in Philadelphia. A well-orga-
nized group in the galleries relentlessly
chanting "We want Willkie" turned the delegate tide in his favor.

Precedents have been set. In 1932, Democrat Franklin D. Roosevelt became the first to
appear at the convention to accept the nomination. And in the thirties, when air travel was

relatively new and awesome to many, Roosevelt stirred excitement as he flew in from
New York City to Chicago to do so.

The 1900 Republican convention was
noteworthy because of its selection of a vice-
presidential candidate. President William
McKinley was renominated to run for a second
term. Vice-President Garret A. Hobart had
died in 1899. Party leaders persuaded McKinley to run with Governor Theodore Roosevelt
of New York, a maverick reformer the bosses
wanted to tuck out of sight and action in the
second highest office for four years. The

Do You Know?
1. What are the Constitutional requirements for President?
2. What does the term "smoke-filled room" refer to?
3. Which Socialist Party leader ran in every presidential election from 1928 to 1948?
4. What is the term used when voters registered in one party vote for nominees of another party, as in primary elections?
5. Which primary is the first held each election year?
6. What is a "bandwagon effect"?
7. What is a dark-horse nominee?
8. What state first made the primary mandatory on a statewide basis?
9. What is "clout"?
10. Which nominee for President had the follow-ing slogan, symbol, or campaign style?
    a. "I Like Ike"
    b. a shoe with a hole in the sole
    c. "Clean Gene"
    d. the sunflower
    e. "Cross of Gold" speech
    f. "Tippecanoe and Tyler, Too"
    g. "We're Ready for Teddy"

Answers: (1) natural-born citizen, at least 35 years old, a U.S. resident for 14 years; (2) especially at political con-ventions, meetings of influential politicians in private to plan strategy or to agree on nominees; (3) Norman Thomas; (4) crossover voting; (5) the New Hampshire primary; (6) a big win that may influence voters else-where to support a nominee; (7) a person unexpectedly nominated for political office; (8) Wisconsin—the law was approved by referendum in 1904; (9) power, espe-cially political power; (10a) Dwight Eisenhower; (10b) Adlai Stevenson; (10c) Eugene McCarthy; (10d) Alfred Landon; (10e) William Jennings Bryan; (10f) William H. Harrison; (10g) Edward Kennedy.

*A cartoonist criticizes President Theodore Roosevelt's efforts to choose
his successor, William Howard Taft, then secretary of war.*

strategy backfired upon McKinley's assassination in 1901. Roosevelt became President.

When the Democratic convention convened in Los Angeles in July 1960, the time
for decision had come. It would be com-
pressed into only a few days of feverish activity. The candidates and their followers
knew there would be little rest for anyone.

On Monday, July 11, for example, John
Kennedy appeared before nine state caucuses

between 8:30 A.M. and 1:30 P.M. His afternoon
was just as full, and so were the next two
days. Johnson and Symington, their aides,
and Stevenson's were equally occupied.
Wavering delegates had to be kept in camp.
More votes had to be won away from rival
factions.

The Stevenson group provided one high
point of excitement at Los Angeles before
names were placed in nomination and ballot-

President Wilson's 1916 re-election campaign truck bore his "Peace with Honor" pledge and reminders of achievements in his first term.

ing began on Wednesday, July 13. Persuasive Stevenson supporters managed to split the California delegation on Tuesday, gaining 31½ votes for their candidate. Following this achievement, Stevenson people in the convention hall stepped up their demonstrations. On Wednesday evening, Stevenson delegates and his followers who had packed the spectator galleries erupted in demonstration upon his nomination. To some people, it appeared that the 1940 performance in Philadelphia that had landed the nomination for Wendell Willkie might be repeated.

Actually, the possibility was remote. Stevenson knew that he needed the endorsement of his home state of Illinois if his candidacy was to succeed, so on Wednesday afternoon he had asked Mayor Richard J. Daley of Chicago, the leader of the Illinois delegation, if he could count on greater Illinois support. The state had caucused earlier, casting 59½ votes for Kennedy, 2 for Stevenson. When Daley replied no to Stevenson, any hope for his nomination vanished, hours before the frenzy in the convention hall began.

On Wednesday morning, Kennedy appeared to have about 740 votes. But he was still short of a majority, so members of his group kept up the pressure.

Alabama led off the balloting on Wednesday night. That state gave Johnson 20, Kennedy and Symington 3½ each, and Stevenson ½. After Illinois had voted, Kennedy held 100; after Massachusetts, 300; and more than 650 after Pennsylvania. A total of 748 delegate votes—thirteen short of the 761 needed—rested in the Kennedy column as Wyoming was called. All 15 votes from that state went to Kennedy, and the battle for the Democratic nomination was over. The final tally read Kennedy 806, Johnson 409, Symington 86, and Stevenson 79½.

A Democratic vice-presidential candidate was to be nominated on Thursday. There was much speculation on who it might be. Much of the talk centered on Lyndon Johnson, but few people thought he would accept the position if Kennedy offered it to him. Johnson appeared to share the opinion once voiced to him by a fellow Texan and former Vice-President, John Nance Garner, who reportedly said that the vice-presidency was not worth a pitcher of warm spit.

Kennedy was convinced that Johnson, a Southerner, would be valuable in attracting votes in November and giving the ticket geographic balance. So he offered Johnson the vice-presidency. After several hours' consultation with advisers, Johnson took it. On July 14, the convention endorsed Johnson by acclamation.

There was no suspense about the Republican nominee as about 2,600 delegates and alternates trooped to that party's convention in Chicago later in July 1960. A dispute over the party platform seemed possible, however.

On June 8, Nelson Rockefeller had loosed a blast at what he considered the lack of proper Republican attention to national defense, civil rights, the economy, welfare, education, and other issues. From Rockefeller's point of view, the Eisenhower Administration had drifted, addressing itself to foreign and domestic problems only as they arose. This stance had a decidedly disturbing effect on intraparty relations.

Eisenhower, along with more conservative party leaders, resented what they considered to be Rockefeller's interference. In writing the party platform, the platform committee ignored a number of Rockefeller's points, and on others it did not go nearly so far as he would have liked.

Wishing to quiet factional strife, Nixon hurried to New York City to meet Rockefeller as the convention gathered. There the two came to agreement along lines that Rockefeller demanded. Now a bitter floor fight over the platform loomed, but Nixon managed to sell party leaders in Chicago on what was called the "Compact of Fifth Avenue."

Without further tussling, the Chicago convention nominated Nixon for the presidency. As Nixon's running mate, the delegates chose Henry Cabot Lodge of Massachusetts, whom Kennedy had defeated for a Massachusetts Senate seat in 1952.

Third Parties

Nixon and Kennedy were not the only ones in the 1960 presidential race. Although they posed no threat to the major parties, more than a dozen others joined, among them nominees representing the Conservative Party of Virginia, the Prohibition Party, Socialist Workers Party, the National States' Rights Party, the Vegetarian Party, the Conservative Party of New Jersey, the Socialist Labor Party, the Tax Cut Party, and the Greenback Party.

The history of third parties is long, and their presence has had social and political significance. The Anti-Masonic group began it all by challenging the major organizations in the 1820's and the early 1830's. By 1860, the Anti-Masonic movement had dissolved, but the third party spirit lived on. Slavery was then a vital issue, and the campaign featured a four-way race. The Democrats split into two factions—Northern Democrats and Southern Democrats. A small group of politicians formed a third party—the Constitutional Union Party. Opposing these three parties was the Republican Party, led by Abraham Lincoln.

During the 1870's, the Greenback Party flourished, and the Populist, or People's, Party grew out of the Greenback movement. In the early 1890's, the country suffered from economic depression, with farmers wilting under the burden of low prices and mortgage foreclosures when they could not pay their debts. Populism—support for the needs and rights of the common people—swept the Midwest and much of the South, and in 1892 the Populists nominated James B. Weaver, an old Greenbacker, for President. Weaver pulled more than a million popular votes and 22 electoral votes, and several Populists won seats in Congress.

The Populist movement's chief significance lay in its long-range influence. Among other things, Populists called for the free coinage of silver to increase the money supply; government ownership of railroad, telephone, and telegraph systems; direct election of U.S. senators; a federal income tax; and an eight-hour workday. The Democrats adopted the silver plank in 1896, and eventually absorbed the Populist Party. Many of the changes that group demanded came to pass in later years.

The history of the Populist Party illustrates the value of third parties in U.S. political history. Although they have won no national elections, the third parties have often forced the major parties to adopt or support important new issues.

In 1920, the right to vote was assured for women when the 19th Amendment to the Constitution was ratified.

A third-party movement split the Republicans in 1912. Theodore Roosevelt, dissatisfied with his chosen successor, William Howard Taft, sought to regain the presidency that year. Regular Republicans stayed with Taft, so Roosevelt led the Progressive Party, also called the Bull Moose Party. With the Republicans split, Democrat Woodrow Wilson won the election.

Robert M. La Follette, a Republican, led a splinter independent party in 1924, but he carried only one state, Wisconsin. A more serious challenge within the Democratic Party arose in 1948. Henry Wallace, Vice-President under Franklin D. Roosevelt and secretary of commerce under Harry S. Truman, headed a left-wing Progressive Party that year. In addition, Southerners dissatisfied with the Democratic stand on civil rights formed their own ticket behind Senator Strom Thurmond of South Carolina. Truman, the regular Democratic candidate, won the presidency, however.

In 1992, H. Ross Perot, a Texas billionaire, entered the presidential race as an independent candidate. Perot received approximately 20 per cent of the popular vote. However, he failed to get a single electoral vote. In 1996, Perot ran again as the nominee of the Reform Party, which he had founded. He again failed to win.

After a severe economic downturn in 2008, a number of conservative political activist groups formed a loose connection that came to be called the "tea party movement." The group opposed the economic policies of President Barack Obama. The group had no formal structure or leader. However, in November 2010, victories by a number of candidates supported by the tea party helped the Republicans take control of the U.S. House of Representatives.

Campaigning Nominees

The life of presidential nominees once was relatively tranquil. In the early days of the Republic, they seldom appeared in public. It was judged unseemly for an aspirant to seek votes openly.

Stephen A. Douglas of Illinois, the regular Democratic nominee in the four-way race in 1860, discarded that tradition. Douglas traveled thousands of miles or kilometers in the Midwest, South, and the East making campaign speeches.

No one followed that example, however, until William Jennings Bryan stumped in 1896. Bryan campaigned even more extensively than Douglas, on some days giving more than two dozen speeches, many of them at "whistle stops"—places where trains stop only on request. After Bryan's performance, presidential nominees traveled, appeared, and made speeches, no longer disguising their quest for votes.

The hoopla that accompanies a campaign today—slogans, songs, parades, buttons, banquets, and picnics, for example—dates mainly to the Whig campaign of 1840. The country was in an economic depression then, but the Whigs did not wish to discuss the economy or any other issue. They nominated William Henry Harrison, hero of the Battle of Tippecanoe in 1811 and of the War of 1812. The Whigs balanced their ticket with a former Democrat, John Tyler of Virginia. Then they amused the voters with parades, songs, and the slogan "Tippecanoe and Tyler Too." In the "Log Cabin and Hard Cider" campaign, they portrayed opponent Martin Van Buren as an aristocrat and Harrison as one of the common people. Harrison won.

The advent of the jet, squeezing hours from travel time, made presidential campaigning even more frantic. Nominees now are expected to be in more places, and despite the availability of television as a means to communicate with the electorate, nominees believe they must appear in the flesh to seek votes. A presidential race to-day is exhausting, especially for nominees who have just finished grueling primary battles like the ones in 1960.

When Congress returned to session after the 1960 conventions, a restless Senator Kennedy was pinned in Washington. Vice-President Nixon was free to move, and within 10 days of his nomination he had appeared in several states. Having pledged to visit all 50, he ultimately kept his promise, gathering in the final ones during a 7,170-mile (11,539-kilometer) jet trip in the final hours of the campaign. According to Republican reports, Nixon flew 65,500 miles (105,412 kilometers) in all, making at least one appearance in 188 cities, delivering 150 major—and innumerable minor—speeches, and appearing before an estimated 10 million persons.

The Kennedy campaign proved as hectic as Nixon's. Kennedy chose to concentrate his greatest efforts in California and in the large industrial states of the Midwest and East, which held many electoral votes. He would not neglect other parts of the nation, but in Texas and the South in general, he would leave most of the campaigning to his running mate, Lyndon Johnson.

A vital member of the Kennedy campaign team was Louis Harris, whose business was polling public opinion. During the 1960 campaign, Harris would add a new dimension to electioneering, sounding out for political purposes the attitudes and opinions of more people in America than ever before.

Public opinion polls concerning elections probably date to 1824, when the editor of the *Harrisburg Pennsylvanian* asked a number of people in Wilmington, Del., who they thought would win the Presidency that year. On the basis of the figures he gathered, the editor predicted victory for Andrew Jackson. Jackson won the most popular votes, but he failed to get a majority of electoral votes. The House of Representatives then elected John Quincy Adams President.

Over the years, many newspapers relied on straw votes—rather casual voter surveys—to predict election winners. Not until the 1930's did concerted and consistent efforts at polling emerge. In 1936, *Literary Digest* magazine grievously miscalculated public opinion. On the basis of a poll, it predicted that Alfred M. Landon of Kansas would defeat president Franklin D. Roosevelt. But Roosevelt won re-election in a landslide.

The magazine's error lay in its sample—that is, the individuals it questioned. The *Digest* had mailed 10 million questionnaires to addresses gathered from telephone directories. Two million were returned. There were relatively few phones in rural areas then, and depression times made phone service unaffordable for many families in other areas. But poor voters could cast their ballots as well as prosperous ones. The *Literary Digest* had based its conclusions on a badly skewed sample.

Although polltakers had achieved a somewhat sounder scientific basis for their efforts by 1948, they erred badly that year, too. All polls predicted that Thomas E. Dewey would defeat President Harry S. Truman. The pollsters were so confident of the results that they stopped asking questions in October. There rested their biggest mistake. Support for Truman grew in the closing days of the campaign, and he went on to win in an upset.

Polltaking today produces fairly accurate results. Polls correctly and regularly forecast presidential election returns within a few percentage points. The pollsters are now a vital part of any major election campaign.

In addition to testing a politician's popularity, they also seek information on voters' attitudes on issues. These results, along with the list of items a nominee stresses during a campaign, frequently guide governmental policy.

Richard Nixon stressed the Eisenhower record, promising to do even better. He emphasized the peace and the general prosperity that Americans had experienced during President Eisenhower's years in the White House.

Kennedy concentrated on issues such as the recession, from which the nation was only gradually recovering, and what he termed a "missile gap" the Eisenhower Administration had allegedly allowed to develop in military preparedness. Kennedy labeled the administration as stodgy and self-satisfied, promising that he would "get the country moving again."

Nixon emphasized his years in government on a policy-making level, coming down on his opponent's youth and lack of experience. This contrast remained in the minds of many voters until the first television debate, one of four historic campaign confrontations.

Here was something new. Presidential nominees in the past had seldom met face-to-face. But in 1960, Kennedy and Nixon appeared together on television before a total audience variously estimated at from 85 million to 120 million persons. Four meetings were arranged. The first, in Chicago on Sept. 26, 1960, focused on domestic issues.

The debate rules called for each nominee to make an opening statement, answer questions from reporters chosen to participate, respond to the other nominee's replies, and wind up with a closing statement. Each segment was rigidly timed.

At the close of the first debate, opinions on who had "won" differed. To many people who had listened on radio, the nominees seemed about even. Television viewers seemed to disagree. Among those polled afterward in one survey, 39 per cent granted Kennedy victory and 23 per cent chose Nixon. That left 38 per cent undecided.

To many viewers, Nixon seemed nervous, somewhat unsure. But Kennedy came across as relaxed, confident, and mature, quick with facts and ideas in his responses. Perhaps more than anything else, the first TV debate destroyed the image of Kennedy as immature and inexperienced.

In subsequent debates Nixon repaired whatever damage he had suffered in the first, and according to one poll he was chosen winner of the third by 42 to 39 per cent. A Roper Poll reported that 57 per cent of those who voted in November said that the meetings had influenced their decisions. Among a

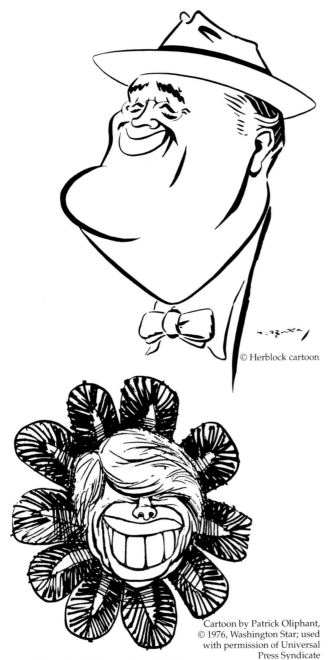

© Herblock cartoon

Cartoon by Patrick Oliphant, © 1976, Washington Star; used with permission of Universal Press Syndicate

Wide smiles of Roosevelt and Carter were lampooned in political cartoons.

Roper sample representing 4 million voters who said that the debates alone had made their decisions, 26 per cent had voted for Nixon, 72 per cent for Kennedy.

The 1960 Cliffhanger

A Gallup Poll taken right after the Democratic convention showed Kennedy with a 52 per cent to 48 per cent lead over Nixon. After Nixon began his campaign in August, the lead switched to 53 per cent to 47 per cent in Nixon's favor. Then, with the election three

weeks away, the figures favored Kennedy, 49 to 46, with 5 per cent undecided. By election day the difference had narrowed.

The entry of President Eisenhower into the campaign on Nixon's behalf may have helped him. During the last week of the campaign, Eisenhower appeared in Pittsburgh, Cleveland, and New York City. In addition, during the final days the Republicans conducted a television blitz of advertising and Nixon appearances, in some of which President Eisenhower participated.

The Nov. 8, 1960, election results proved closer than they had been in any race since 1884 when Democrat Grover Cleveland defeated Republican James G. Blaine by barely 23,000 popular votes. And the outcome in 1960 was uncertain until well into the morning of November 9.

The final tally gave Kennedy 34,227,096 popular votes to Nixon's 34,107,646, a 49.7 to 49.6 per cent split. Only 119,450 votes separated the two.

The Electoral College assembled in December. When the electors cast their ballots, the results showed Kennedy the victor by a good margin. He had won 23 states with 303 electoral votes. Nixon took 26 states but gained only 219 electoral votes. Fifteen electors in Mississippi, Oklahoma, and Alabama cast their ballots for Senator Harry F. Byrd of Virginia.

The popular-vote margin in several states had been narrow, Kennedy winning in 12 with a bare 2 per cent majority. A shift of a few thousand votes in Illinois and other highly populated states, which have many electoral votes, could have made Richard Nixon President.

The close of the 1960 election came when, in accordance with the U.S. Constitution, the lists of the electoral votes were sent under seal to Washington, D.C. At a joint session of both houses of Congress in January 1961, Vice-President Nixon, as president of the U.S. Senate, opened the certificates. Four tellers—one Democrat and one Republican from each house—counted the votes. John F. Kennedy, who received the majority, was declared elected.

The 1960 election was memorable in many ways. Filled with suspense, it riveted the nation's attention into the wee hours of election night. At 43, John F. Kennedy became the youngest person ever elected President. Leaving the White House at age 71 in 1961,

An upset victory for Harry S. Truman in 1948. The joke is on the Chicago Daily Tribune, which prematurely published this headline.

Eisenhower was the oldest in office up to that time.

The election showed that a Catholic could become President. It marked the passage of the generation of Presidents born in the late 1800's. It was the first time that a sitting senator had vaulted to the highest office since Harding in 1920. And Kennedy became the first candidate from New England to win the presidency since Calvin Coolidge in 1924.

Television, along with jet travel and frequent candidate appearances, made the 1960 campaign the most expensive to date. More important, by 1960 many more people relied on television for impressions and news than on newspapers. Also by 1960, population shifts had made suburbs important ground

for campaigning. And that year more people voted than ever before—64.5 per cent of those eligible.

Finally, the 1960 campaign showed what primaries, plus careful attention to organization in nonprimary states, can do for a relatively unknown candidate. Not long after that, the trend in the number of states holding primaries began to climb. The total was more than 20 in 1972 and rose to 30 by 1976. More states came in before the next presidential election. In 1976, nearly three-fourths of the Democratic delegates and more than two-thirds of the Republicans were chosen in primary elections. That was also the year in which success in primaries changed one candidate from "Jimmy Who?" to President Jimmy Carter.

Primaries have catapulted unknown candidates such as Carter into the political limelight, but they have also provided tests of popularity for well-known candidates—even Presidents considering running for another term. In 1968, Senator Eugene McCarthy of Minnesota, an opponent of U.S. involvement in Vietnam, ran in New Hampshire against President Lyndon B. Johnson, who had come under severe criticism for his Vietnam policies. McCarthy won 42 percent of the vote; Johnson won 48 percent. Some people believe that McCarthy's strong showing became a factor in Johnson's decision not to seek reelection that year.

The Future of Primaries

Although primaries increase voter participation and provide candidates with information useful to their campaigns, they also create conflict within parties, with candidates from the same party facing off. Moreover, the primary season is long. Beginning in New Hampshire, it lasts from late winter into spring. The primaries cost much money and exact much effort, exhausting candidates and their aides even before the post-convention campaign begins.

The 2008 Democratic primaries were particularly expensive, arduous, and historic. Senator Barack Obama—the first major African American candidate for the presidency—did not capture the nomination from Senator Hillary Clinton—the first major woman candidate—until the final primaries on June 3. Even so, he still needed the pledged support of a number of so-called superdelegates—party leaders who could vote for a candidate regardless of the results of their state's primary election or caucus.

Senator Hillary Clinton of New York and Senator Barack Obama of Illinois participate in a televised debate during the historic Democratic primary of 2008.

In most elections, primaries attract relatively few voters. Out of a possible 60 million Democrats in 1976 and half that many Republicans in 30 states, fewer than 30 million cast primary ballots that year. More than 81 million voters, 54 per cent of the electorate, voted in the 1976 general election. Changes in primary election procedures have been suggested. For example, one calls for holding all state primaries the same day.

Changes have already occurred in campaign financing. Although the 1960 campaign was the most expensive in American history up to that time, later runs for the presidency dwarfed it. So far as anyone knows, George Washington did not spend any money getting elected. By contrast, in 1972, all candidates spent a total of more than $137 million. In 1984, Ronald Reagan spent nearly $26 million. In 2004, George W. Bush spent more than $268 million on his election to the presidency.

As campaign war chests swelled, concern over the possibility of rich persons or organizations "buying" elections brought new laws. These sought to regulate campaign spending more closely and to even things out by aiding candidates with public money.

One law in the 1970's permitted federal income taxpayers to deduct a dollar from the sum they paid, to be placed in a fund to provide public campaign money. Another required detailed reporting of contributions and expenses.

A later law limited the amounts of money that individuals and groups could contribute and placed a ceiling on total spending. For primary campaigns, the government now matches private contributions for candidates who raise at least $100,000 on their own in amounts of $5,000 in each of 20 states, limiting individual contributions to no more than $250 each. Federal money is available on a matching basis for general elections, too.

Congress established the Federal Election Commission in 1975 to oversee fund-raising and spending. The President appoints the six members of the group, no more than three of whom may belong to the same political party.

A 1976 ruling by the Supreme Court of the United States held that a candidate who does not accept public money need not stay within spending limits. Moreover, limits on what a group can contribute have led to the formation of many "political action committees," or PAC's, each of which can raise and contribute money. In 2008, Barack Obama became the first major candidate to decline public financing. He raised over $745 million for his campaign.

In the 1990's and early 2000's, many proposals were made by Congress to reform the way political campaigns are financed. The proposals included limiting or banning efforts by PAC's, banning unregulated and unlimited contributions, limiting certain kinds of advertisement, and setting spending limits for political candidates.

Aftermath of the 1960 Race

In choosing members of his government, President John F. Kennedy appointed Adlai Stevenson as U.S. ambassador to the United Nations. Stevenson held that post until his death in 1965. Two other rivals for the 1960 nomination, Hubert Humphrey and Stuart Symington, remained in the Senate.

The Kennedy Administration endured fewer than three years. Kennedy was assassinated in Dallas on Nov. 22, 1963, and Lyndon B. Johnson became President.

In 1964, the Democrats nominated Johnson, and he easily won election in his own right, defeating Senator Barry Goldwater of Arizona. Johnson's running mate that year was Humphrey.

After Johnson pulled himself out of the race in 1968, the Democrats nominated Humphrey. Making a political comeback, Richard M. Nixon won the Republican nomination and beat Humphrey by a narrow margin. Four years later, Nixon posted a much greater victory over Senator George McGovern of South Dakota.

Stuart Symington ran for the Senate for the last time in 1972. He retired at the end of that term. Lyndon Johnson died in 1973. In that same year, Vice-President Spiro Agnew resigned while under criminal investigation. In accord with the 25th Amendment to the Constitution, Nixon appointed Representative Gerald R. Ford of Michigan to the vice-presidency.

Nixon's Administration fell in 1974 because of the Watergate scandal. Facing possible impeachment for his involvement in the scandal, Nixon resigned the presidency on Aug. 9, 1974. He died in 1994.

Ford then became President. He appointed Nelson Rockefeller, who had resigned as governor of New York in 1973, as Vice-President. Rockefeller retired from politics after his term as Vice-President ended in 1977. He died in 1979.

A car separates Republicans from Democrats as they argue about the 2000 election in Palm Beach County, Florida.

A Photo Finish

The election in 2000 turned out to be the closest one since the cliffhanger of 1960. Opinion polls showed George W. Bush slightly ahead of Al Gore after both conventions were over, but the numbers were close enough that there was no clear leader. Many political analysts predicted that the popular vote totals would be exceptionally close but that Bush would be slightly ahead in the popular vote while Gore could manage to win the electoral vote.

As the election results came in on November 7, the race seemed to be as close as expected. But a strange thing became apparent as the night went on—Gore pulled slightly ahead in the popular vote, but as state after state was called in favor of Bush, his chances to win a majority of the electoral votes seemed slimmer.

Eventually, both men had enough electoral votes that winning Florida would be the ticket to winning the election. Early in the evening, major news networks had projected that Gore would take Florida, but later they retracted that projection because Bush was pulling ahead in the vote count.

Early in the morning of November 8, news reports began indicating that Bush would win Florida. But just before he was going to make his presidential acceptance speech, his projected Florida win was retracted because his lead had dropped significantly as more votes were counted.

For the first time since 1876, the people of the United States didn't know who was going to be their next president the day after election day. The initial results of Florida's vote count had been so close—Bush had a lead of 1,784 votes out of more than 6 million votes cast—that Florida law required a recount. After the automatic recount and overseas ballots were counted, Bush's lead had dwindled to a mere 930 votes.

Because the election was so close, Gore asked for a manual recount of ballots in some counties, hoping to pick up enough votes to win. While the votes were being counted by hand, Bush sued to get the manual recounts stopped. As Gore and Bush battled in the courts about the manual recounting, members of the two parties became more and more emotional about the election. Many people, especially in Florida, began staging rallies and protests.

Each defeat in the legal battles resulted in an appeal, moving the issue rapidly through the court systems. One ruling allowed results from some of the manual recounts to be included in the certified results of Florida's totals, but Bush still maintained a lead of 537 votes.

In only a few weeks, the matter ended up in the Supreme Court. With the constitutional deadline for states to finalize their electoral voters looming overhead, the Supreme Court ruled that the recounts should stop. The highest court of the land ruling against Gore convinced him to concede. In speeches on December 13, 2000, both Bush and Gore called for their parties to come together and unify the nation behind Bush as the United States 43rd President.

Moving into the White House

From the West Front of the Capitol, one looks out across a statue of Ulysses S. Grant on horseback at the foot of the Hill toward the Mall, flanked by Constitution and Independence avenues, trisected by Madison and Jefferson drives. In the near distance, the imposing shaft of the Washington Monument dominates the landscape. Beyond that lies the Reflecting Pool, before the Lincoln Memorial, which overlooks the Potomac River. This was the scene upon which George W. Bush gazed as he prepared to take the oath of office as 43rd President of the United States on Saturday, Jan. 20, 2001.

The Inauguration—A National Celebration

As George W. Bush prepared to assume the presidency from President Clinton on Saturday, January 20, 2001, a cold, steady drizzle fell from the Washington, D.C., skies and the temperature was slowly plummeting. As it turned out, the bad weather played a major role in the day's proceedings. While a 700,000-person crowd was predicted to attend, far fewer actually braved the elements.

Inauguration Day 2001 marked not only the beginning of the 43rd presidency, it ended one of the nation's most hotly disputed presidential elections in history. Bush was finally declared victorious over Al Gore 36 days after the actual election. The high emotion of the election was still evident throughout inauguration day, as thousands of protesters voiced their opposition of the new President, his views, and the election process.

George and Laura Bush began Inauguration Day with a church service at St. John's Episcopal Church on Washington's Lafayette Square. Afterward, they were whisked away to the White House to join outgoing President Clinton for coffee.

Kentucky Republican Senator Mitch McConnell, chairman of the Congressional Committee on Inaugural Ceremonies, called the ceremony to order at 11:30 a.m. The Reverend Franklin Graham offered the inaugural invocation. Soon after, Vice-President-elect Dick Cheney was sworn into office by Chief Justice William Rehnquist. Shortly after noon, Rehnquist administered the oath of office to Bush.

After his swearing in, Bush delivered his inaugural address. In his speech, he thanked President Clinton for his eight years of service and Gore for an election campaign that was "conducted in spirit and ended in grace." And he promised that his administration would embody "a new commitment to live out our nation's promise through civility, courage, compassion, and character."

Throughout the ceremony, onlookers seated on the Capitol grounds tried to stay warm and dry by sitting on their hands, huddling close together, or wearing plastic, disposable rain ponchos.

Soon after becoming President, Bush made his way from the Capitol to the White House. From the lawn of his new residence, he watched the inaugural parade held in his honor from a grandstand. With him were First Lady Laura Bush, Vice-President Dick Cheney, and his wife, Lynne. The inaugural parade is a tradition that dates back to 1801, when Thomas Jefferson rode a horse from Congress's house to the President's house after his swearing in.

Despite the continuing drizzle and wind, thousands of spectators watched the traditional and patriotic parade. The U.S. Marine Band kicked it off with its rendition of the U.S. Marine Corps Hymn. The parade's first float, "Celebrating America's Spirit Together," rolled its way down the street with entertainer Wayne Newton aboard. Following behind were some 40 marching bands, including bands from President Bush's and Vice-President Cheney's home states, and various other floats. "Old Glory," an eagle-bearing float, ended the parade.

Eight inaugural balls were scheduled to begin within two hours of the end of the parade—around 5 p.m. The balls have been part of the inauguration ceremonies since 1809 and have been held every four years since Dwight and Mamie Eisenhower restored the tradition after a 36-year absence in 1953. President Bush and First Lady Laura Bush danced through all eight events, spending just a few minutes at each one, thanking ball-goers for their support. Bush wore a black tuxedo and the first lady wore a sparkling red gown. Vice-President Dick Cheney also made the rounds. At each ball, bands played "Hail to the Chief" for Bush and "Hail Columbia" for Cheney. Entertainment for the balls included the Guy Lombardo Orchestra, Meat Loaf, Kelsey Grammer, Drew Carey, the Tommy Dorsey Orchestra, and Nell Carter.

Page 74: *Moving into the most famous U.S. home, the White House.*

Pennsylvania Avenue on Lincoln's Inaugural Day, 1861. Sharp-shooters were posted in trees to protect the President-elect.

Just hours before leaving office, outgoing President Clinton pardoned more than 130 people, including Whitewater figure Susan McDougal, former Housing Secretary Henry Cisneros, ex-CIA chief Don Deutch, publishing heiress Patty Hearst, and his brother Roger Clinton. Some of his pardons would raise eyebrows in the coming weeks. Also before leaving office, Clinton designated another monument, the Governors Island National Monument, in New York City, and announced the release of a $100 million to fund 1,400 additional police officers. And in keeping with tradition, Clinton left a handwritten note for his successor on his desk in the Oval Office. These notes, which are not usually made public, are said to include words of encouragement and advice.

Clinton left Washington, D.C., shortly after the presidency transferred to Bush. He attended an emotional goodbye ceremony at Andrews Air Force Base in Maryland, where he reminisced in public about his time in office: "You gave me the ride of my life," he told onlookers, "and I tried to give as good as I got." The youngest former president since Theodore Roosevelt then boarded a flight to New York City.

Tour from Mount Vernon

The first President's inaugural address took about the same amount of time as George W.

Bush's—20 minutes. George Washington delivered it in New York City, however, for in 1789, there was no city of Washington in the District of Columbia. New York was serving as the capital at the time.

For George Washington, the journey to New York was a tiring though triumphal tour. Admirers at Alexandria, Va., and Baltimore tendered him dinners. A company of citizens on horseback, along with cannoneers firing salutes, saw him off from Baltimore at 5:30 a.m. Horseback riders escorted the President's carriage from Wilmington, Del., to the Pennsylvania line. There another mounted troupe took him to Chester, Pa. Washington then changed from his carriage to a white horse to ride the 15 miles (24 kilometers) into Philadelphia.

At least 20,000 cheering persons spread out from the bridge over the Schuylkill River to the center of town to welcome him. There, after a banquet at the City Tavern, Washington enjoyed a fireworks show.

The new President passed under an arch of flowers erected in his honor at Trenton, N.J., an old Revolutionary War battleground for him. At the New Jersey shore, he boarded a decorated barge that would take him past Staten Island to Manhattan. Many ships fell in behind Washington's barge, and, as a battery on Staten Island opened a 13-gun salute, all ships broke out flags. Once the President's barge landed at Murray's Wharf, at the foot of Wall Street, a carriage took

Washington to the first President's home, on Cherry Street.

Washington's inauguration took place a week later. Thirteen cannon roars opened the day on April 30. Dressed in a brown coat and knee breeches made in Connecticut, wearing white silk stockings and shoes with silver buckles, Washington waited at his residence as noon approached. At last, the Congressional delegation arrived to escort him to the place of inauguration, Federal Hall, where Congress met. Washington buckled on his sword and, outside on Cherry Street, entered a large coach to pass through streets thronged with a crowd of well-wishers.

Members of the House and Senate meeting together received Washington at Federal Hall. John Adams, who had been sworn in as Vice-President in the Senate chamber before Washington's arrival, then led him through a windowed door out onto a small balcony overlooking Wall Street. Gazing out, Washington saw people everywhere, jammed into the streets, filling every rooftop in sight.

Washington took a position close to the railing. He raised one hand, placing his other on a Bible resting on a cushion. It was held by an attendant described as a "small short." Washington listened as Robert R. Livingston, chancellor of the state of New York, intoned the same oath all the Presidents who have since followed Washington have spoken. Then, though the attendant held it as high as possible, the first President, who was well over six feet (183 centimeters) tall, still had to bend deeply to kiss the Bible.

With that, Livingston addressed the crowd below: "It is done. Long live George Washington, President of the United States!" The people responded with a roar. In the harbor, cannons boomed, drowning out the city's pealing church bells. George Washington then read his inaugural address inside.

After the ceremony, the President attended St. Paul's Chapel. He enjoyed a quiet dinner at home, then appeared at two receptions and was on hand for more fireworks. There was no inaugural ball in 1789. That feature of the President's first day in office did not appear until March 4, 1809, when the James Madison Administration began.

By then, the capital had moved to its permanent location in Washington, D.C. Madison's ball was a hot and crowded affair at Long's Hotel, the present site of the Library of Congress. About 400 persons attended. The festivities were only tolerated by the President, but his wife Dolley, who was the first lady of Washington society for the first half of the 19th century, loved it. She wore a sleeveless gown of yellow. Pearls hung around her neck, and she sported a turban—headgear for which she was famous. This creation, of purple velvet and white satin with two bird-of-paradise plumes, came from Paris.

Former President Thomas Jefferson was there, and upon his arrival the band struck up "The Jefferson March." Future President John Quincy Adams also attended. He was one of the few who did not have a good time. Adams found "the crowd excessive, the heat oppressive, and the entertainment bad."

Andrew Jackson was the first President said to have come from the common people. Conservatives feared the rule of the mob when he was elected. As it was, his inauguration in 1829 turned into a wild celebration. Even before the day of his inaugural, he was surrounded by a ragtag group of office seekers.

Jackson, like Jefferson before him, walked to his inauguration. It was held on the East Portico of the Capitol. Monroe's was the first held there, in 1817. About 10,000 to 20,000 people attended Jackson's ceremony.

For all the folderol, Jackson's inaugural speech was low-key, both in its message and the way in which it was delivered. About the presidency Jackson said, "I approach it with trembling reluctance. But my country has willed it, and I obey." This statement was not in keeping with Jackson's tough-as-nails image, which had come across in his campaign and in his earlier career.

Although his speech was judged less than brilliant in its style, Jackson made some important points about the political climate of the country for the next half century. He predicted, for example, a conflict between the state and federal governments, and he asked for the two factions to compromise.

Jackson had no inaugural parade because he was in mourning for his recently deceased wife, Rachel. The reception, immediately following the ceremony, was a nightmare to many folk of the day. In the East Room, where cake, ice cream, and orange punch were served, the crowd rushed in, leaving dignitaries behind.

Reagan gives his inaugural speech, Jan. 20 1981, on the Capitol's west steps.

Women fainted, glasses and china were broken, and clothes were torn.

Margaret Smith, a society matron who witnessed the whole scene, described it as a rabble and a mob, with scrambling, fighting, and romping. According to her account, women fainted and men were seen with bloody noses.

After refreshments were removed, the crowd left. Many dignitaries, including Jackson, had already slipped quietly out.

In 1837, Martin Van Buren had two inaugural balls. One was at Carusi's Assembly Rooms, the other at Gadsby's, at the time Washington's leading hotel. There and at other hotels and boarding houses, many among the out-of-town inaugural crowd had sought places to stay—in vain. A few Bostonians slept the night in the chairs of a barber shop.

Lincoln Incognito

The first Lincoln inaugural on March 4, 1861, although far more subdued, was unique because of the unconventional way the President-elect arrived in Washington, D.C. He was incognito, under the protection of a Scot named Allan Pinkerton, whose name would be famous. Pinkerton was hired by the Philadelphia, Wilmington & Baltimore Railroad to investigate rumors that secessionists were going to disrupt rail service. While on his mission, he uncovered a plot by secessionists to kill the President-elect on his way to the inauguration. Lincoln was already en route.

Lincoln traveled via more than 40 cities and towns between Springfield, Ill., and Washington. At each, he stopped to greet the people and say at least a few words. On the last leg of his journey, at Philadelphia, Pinkerton informed him of the plot against his life. The next day, Washington's Birthday, Lincoln was planning to raise the flag at Philadelphia's Independence Hall. Afterward he was to travel to Harrisburg, Pa.

Pinkerton advised Lincoln to leave Philadelphia immediately for Washington in order to avoid the plotters, who were suspected to be in Baltimore. The change in plans, Pinkerton hoped, would throw the would-be assassins off-guard. Lincoln refused to leave Philadelphia immediately but did agree to slip away from the crowd at Harrisburg at dusk on the next day. He would then board a special train back to Philadelphia. There he transferred to a train going south that night. Once aboard, Lincoln and his party got accommodations in the sleeping car. In this way, he could avoid being seen in Baltimore.

When Lincoln arrived in Washington, he was said to have "crept into" the city like a "thief in the night." Still, he was safe, and the peace had been preserved. According to reports, Lincoln had not feared for his own safety, but he worried about the additional violence that would have occurred had he been harmed.

Lincoln would bravely attempt to cement the ties of the union, but by March 1861 Jefferson Davis had already become the first (and last) president of the Confederacy, and seven Southern States had seceded.

Anything Lincoln would have said at a time when the nation was on the brink of civil war would have been judged important. But Lincoln, an excellent speaker, also held the crowd with his eloquence.

Do You Know?
1. What was the "Peanut Special"?
2. Who was the first President to have an official inaugural ball?
3. What famous detective protected Abraham Lincoln on his inaugural trip to Washington, D.C.?
4. What famous American poet read a poem at the Kennedy inauguration?
5. What first lady remained in the White House more than a month after her husband's assassination?
6. How was the East Room of the White House first used?
7. When did the White House get its first stove?
8. What first lady formed the Fine Arts Committee for the White House?
9. What President hired Louis C. Tiffany to redecorate the White House?
10. How many rooms does the White House have?

Answers: (1) a special train to Carter's inauguration, chartered for the citizens of his hometown in Georgia; (2) Madison; (3) Allan Pinkerton; (4) Robert Frost; (5) Mary Todd Lincoln; (6) to hang the household laundry, during the J. Adams Administration; (7) about 1850, under Fillmore; (8) Jacqueline Kennedy; (9) Arthur; (10) 132.

With sharpshooters positioned in the trees and tension crackling in the air, the new President, standing on a temporary platform above the steps of the East Portico of the Capitol, told his audience that Southern property would not be endangered. He said that the fugitive slave law would be upheld but that the rights of the free blacks should be protected. He also said that he had "no objection" to making the new 13th amendment, which was yet to be ratified, "irrevocable." This amendment, which never was ratified, would have prevented federal interference with slavery in the states where it already existed.

Lincoln said that "the Union of these states is perpetual," and that he as President would fulfill "a simple duty . . . unless . . . the American people . . . in some authoritative manner direct the contrary."

Regarding secession, he said the central idea of seceding was "the essence of anarchy" and that those who ignored the wishes of the majority were asking for chaos or tyranny.

Reactions to Lincoln's speech were mixed but largely predictable. The Southern newspaper *Charleston Mercury* referred to his "insolence" and "brutality," while the *Chicago Tribune* thought Lincoln's speech was free from political clichés and vagueness. The *New York Tribune* praised Lincoln's honesty and directness, and thought the speech showed his ability to be a good President. The *Baltimore Sun* said the speech breathed "the spirit of mischief."

A prominent Southerner, Jubal A. Early of Virginia, said that the inaugural was "a guarantee that Lincoln would perform his duty." John A. Gilmer, another Southerner, asked, what else do Southerners want? These opinions were, however, expressed privately.

The Woodrow Wilsons broke the chain of quadrennial dancing celebrations that had started with Madison. They requested that none be held for them in 1913. Both believed that such events detracted from the dignity and responsibility of the presidential office.

Warren and Florence Harding sought to revive the inaugural ball in 1921. Congress, however, refused to appropriate money for what a majority of its members considered an unnecessary event. So friends of the Hardings, the Edward Beale McLeans, staged a ball for them in their spacious Washington town house. Attended by representatives of the diplomatic corps, Cabinet members, other

Bill Clinton plays tenor saxophone at an inaugural ball on January 19, 1993.

government officials, and Washington socialites, it was a huge success.

"Silent Cal" Coolidge went to bed early on his inauguration night in 1925. He was asleep by 10 p.m. By then inaugural balls had become customary once again, and so they have re-mained until the present.

In 1933, the 20th Amendment made the in-auguration a midwinter event when it changed the date from March 4 to January 20. Franklin D. Roosevelt was the first President sworn in on the new date.

The ceremony through which power is transferred—the inauguration—is a sort of rite of passage the President and the nation share. Inaugurations are also events during which symbols fly thick and fast.

Inaugural Symbols

John F. Kennedy's inauguration took place in 1961. In keeping with modern inaugurals, the festivities spread out over several days. A deep snowfall covered the city the night before the inauguration ceremony, but the weather put no chill on the festivities.

The Kennedys were to be an immensely popular First Couple. Young, vigorous, and cultured, they gave the nation an administration that would be referred to as Camelot. Everywhere at the inaugural and in the events surrounding it were symbols of hope and renewal. Jacqueline even obliged by giving birth to a baby, John, Jr., a few weeks before her husband took office.

Kennedy's inaugural speech was perhaps the most memorable event o his inauguration, especially when he made the now-famous plea: "And so, my fellow Americans, ask not what your country can do for you—ask what you can do for your country."

If Kennedy asked for a new commitment, he also gave one that day. By asking the poet Robert Frost to read one of his poems, Kennedy was paying tribute to the arts and declaring that the life of the mind was important to the nation. Said Frost on being asked to read at the inaugural, "I may not be equal to [the task] but I can accept it for my cause—the arts, poetry, now for the first time taken into the affairs of [state]."

When the 86-year-old Frost rose to read his new poem, he managed but three lines when the bright winter sun blinded him and he could not continue. So he recited an old poem, "The Gift Outright," from memory.

The Jimmy Carter inaugural in 1977 was also full of symbolic gestures, such as the Carters' walk down Pennsylvania Avenue after the swearing in. Most recent Presidents have ridden in limousines, but Carter wished to be with the people, emulating Thomas Jefferson and Andrew Jackson by walking during part of his inaugural ceremonies.

Just as each President has an individual style, so the chief executive also represents the region of the nation. No President in living memory has been so closely associated with one as Carter, who, from Georgia, was from the Deep South.

For the inauguration, Carter brought with him nearly 400 relatives and neighbors from his hometown of Plains, Ga. The *Peanut Special,* a special train, pulled away from the town's depot at 1:00 p.m. on January 19. On the way north, the passengers munched on peanuts and sampled peanut soup, Georgia ham, and Georgia-peach ice cream. When the trip was over, the happy throng had eaten 275 pounds (125 kilograms) of peanuts.

Nine individuals have assumed the position of chief executive with no public display. Presidential death elevated eight to the highest office. John Tyler was the first in 1841. Then came Millard Fillmore in 1850, Andrew Johnson in 1865, Chester Arthur in 1881, Theodore Roosevelt in 1901, Calvin Coolidge in 1923, Harry Truman in 1945, and Lyndon Johnson in 1963. Gerald R. Ford was unique among American Presidents, the only one sworn in due to presidential resignation.

Among these nine, Theodore Roosevelt, Coolidge, Truman, and Lyndon Johnson later won election in their own right. They experienced the normal inaugural ceremony in Washington as their second terms began. Tyler, Fillmore, Andrew Johnson, and Arthur did not. They were not nominated to run for the presidency after the terms they had filled expired.

Nor did Gerald Ford achieve election to the presidency. The Republicans nominated him in 1976, but he lost to Democrat Jimmy Carter in November.

The "Frontier Mansion"

The White House, into which "accidental" and other Presidents move, did not acquire its name officially until the Theodore Roosevelt Administration. It was called that, however, during much of the 19th century. Apparently the term first appeared commonly in print in the 1860's. But officially, until Roosevelt's time, the name was the President's House, then the Executive Mansion.

The house was first ready for occupants in 1800. How smooth the transition has been into it has varied. But the first occupants—John and Abigail Adams—probably had the worst time in terms of adjusting to the physical surroundings.

Spending his first night in the White House on November 2, in a letter to Abigail, who as still at home in Braintree, Mass., President Adams included what is now known as the White House Prayer: "I pray Heaven to bestow the best of blessing on this house and all that shall hereafter inhabit it. May none but wise and honest men ever rule under this roof." Franklin D. Roosevelt had the prayer engraved over the mantel in the State Dining Room.

The Adamses "ruled" as best they could during the last four months of John Adams' term, but they were anything but pleased to be residing in the house. Life in the Federal City was not easy in 1800, and they had to rough it. Abigail's letters about the mansion to her family describe the house and its 18-acre (7-hectare) "wilderness" plot in dismal terms.

The building that Abigail Adams complained about so bitterly was damp, cold, and lacked the conveniences that gentry of the 18th century had come to expect. Furthermore, it was little more than a shell, with no rooms completely finished. There was no running water, and wood was in short supply—even though the area was thick with forests. The problem was that laborers who would be willing to cut and cart the wood were few.

The "frontier mansion" had been designed by James Hoban, a prize-winning architect from Ireland. He had topped the versatile Thomas Jefferson in an open competition. Jefferson, wishing to remain anonymous, had signed his design only with the initials *A. Z.*

Hoban's design was considered the most original at the time. It called for wings to be added when necessary. Its likeness can be seen in houses such as Leinster House in Ireland and the Château de Rastignac in southwest France. The latter has an oval portico such as the one added to the White House in 1824.

The entrance to the Cross Hall, as decorated in 1882 during the Arthur Administration. Louis Tiffany designed the stained glass screen.

The building of the original Executive Mansion was slow-going from the first. It was hard to find laborers to work because slave labor in the area of the new District kept the wages of free workers low.

When Jefferson moved into the mansion in 1801, he had his own ideas about how further construction should be handled. But rather than using Hoban, Jefferson hired his own architect, Benjamin Henry Latrobe, who was the architect of the naval docks in Washington and superintendent of public buildings. In doing so, Jefferson was the first of a long line of Presidents who, largely unrestricted, planned to rebuild and redecorate the house according to their own tastes and budgets, and the funds Congress was willing to appropriate.

Jefferson had had plans for long, columned wings to stretch east and west from the central building. Latrobe complied with Jefferson's wishes regarding this extension. Space was provided with the building of terraces for many necessary additions—offices, stables, an ice house, and storage rooms for wines, coal, and wood. The White House grounds were also cleared of debris and construction equipment, and the main staircase was completed. Latrobe did the foundation work and steps of the North Portico. A water closet was added in the house.

In August 1814, during the Madison Administration, a catastrophe befell the Executive Mansion when the British burned it during the War of 1812. It was left roofless and charred, though the walls remained. All that saved them was a heavy rain that fell the night of the fire.

The Madisons took up residence in Octagon House, an elegant mansion on 18th and E streets. A year later, they moved to a second residence, this time a small, private home at the corner of Pennsylvania Avenue and 19th Street. They never returned as president and first lady to the Executive Mansion.

James Hoban was put in charge of repairing the ruined house immediately after the fire, even though the money from Congress was inadequate to the task. The work went slowly. In the fall of 1817, President Monroe's family finally moved in.

On New Year's Day 1818, the rebuilt Executive Mansion was opened to the public. The occasion was the traditional New Year's Day reception. At this point, the mansion was painted white. In 1824, the South Portico was completed.

Furnishings were a problem. In order to solve it, Monroe sold the government his own furniture. It was a fine collection, mostly in the French style and bought while he served as minister to France. The Monroes also had a sampling of domestic pieces.

To complete White House furnishings, Monroe ordered additional pieces from France for the Oval Drawing Room, a parlor, a card room, and a dining room. From a furniture makers in Georgetown, he bought chairs and sofas.

For the oval room there was gilded Empire furniture from Bellangé of Paris, a 50-candle chandelier, and ornaments of porcelain, silver, gilded silver, and gilded bronze. Only one piece of Bellangé furniture has been in the White House ever since this period, the pier table now in the Entrance Hall.

A Bleak White House

The fate of the White House rests mainly in the hands of Congress. Often Congressional appropriations for furniture and upkeep are tied to the political fortunes of the President. Monroe had bought back part of his own furniture by the time John Q. Adams became President. Congress refused to accommodate Adams, and the mansion remained bleak and partially empty. Adams was even attacked for buying a billiard table and chess set, even though they were bought with his own money.

The White House under Adams had a rural appearance. The clerks who came to work there tied their horses in front of the house. The outside of the building needed a hard coat of stucco, and the work on the North Portico was left incomplete. The wings of the house were also unfinished. Yet the grounds of the mansion were notably improved. They were graded and filled with trees and flowers of every description. Adams liked to walk around the White House grounds, which were fast becoming beautiful. There were fruit trees—apple, pear, apricot, plum, and cherry—flowers, including poppies, mustard, and altheas. There were also catalpa trees, hickory, and black walnuts.

In 1829, when Andrew Jackson's time came to move into the White House, relations were strained between him and outgoing President John Q. Adams. The two had fought for the presidency in the election of 1824. It was decided in the House of Representatives when no contender had received the majority of electoral votes. Jackson, however, had received the most votes in the Electoral College. But the House gave the election to Adams. Jackson came back to defeat him in 1828.

Jackson failed to call on the Adamses before the inaugural festivities in 1829. Adams, always polite, sent Jackson a note saying that the couple would move out whenever Jackson requested. He sent an oral message that the Adamses should take their time. They did not, nor did they attend the Jackson inaugural.

Andrew Jackson was gracious while in the White House, despite criticism in some quarters that he was an ill-bred frontier dweller. During his administration, the long-delayed work on the North Portico was completed and the East Room was furnished for the first time.

Martin Van Buren, the next President, suffered more in the White House than Jackson at the hands of political enemies. Van Buren was called a high liver, even though he actually spent less than his predecessor. In 1840, Charles Ogle, a representative from Pennsylvania, criticized Van Buren's "fancy ways" in the famous "Gold Spoon Speech" before the House of Representatives. Speaking as if Van Buren were in the chamber at the time, Ogle said: "[The Executive Mansion] glitters with all imaginable luxuries and gaudy ornaments. . . . I put it to the free citizens of this country . . . will they longer feel inclined to

The White House Executive Office during the late 1890's, when plans for expanding the building were considered.

support their chief servant in a palace as splendid as that of the Caesars, and as richly adorned as the proudest Asiatic mansion?"

Unfortunately for Van Buren, the campaign against his so-called excesses was effective. William Henry Harrison was installed in his place at the Executive Mansion in 1841. Harrison, who died of pneumonia one month after taking office, was unable to prove that his lifestyle was as simple as advertised in his "log cabin and hard cider" campaign.

President John Tyler, Vice-President under Harrison, also had a bleak mansion in which to live. Because of the shortage of money available for upkeep and redecoration, the Executive Mansion had become shabby, according to witnesses at the time. The next residents, the Polks, saw improvements when Congress allocated funds for furnishings. Victorian pieces in rich colors were selected.

There were some new conveniences added in the 1840's. A "refregrator," or icebox, made its debut in 1845, and the heating system was replaced. Apparently, 12 fireplaces Hoban added in 1817 and a furnace put in by President Van Buren were inadequate to take off the winter chill. A gas line was installed in 1848. In June 1849, a carpet was placed in a water closet.

James Buchanan, who presided over an impending civil war, was fortunate in Congressional appropriations for White House improvements. In 1857 Congress gave him $5,000 to buy portraits of five former Presidents and $20,000 for a new conservatory, or greenhouse. Also during the Buchanan Administration, the Blue Room, where Monroe's furniture stood, was redecorated in rococo-revival, a style popular during this period. Only Monroe's Bellangé pier table was not replaced.

Lincoln's time in the White House was a turbulent one both for the President and his house. Some still judged the furniture shabby. Mary Lincoln bought rosewood furniture, velvet hassocks, and brocatelle fabrics, which are similar to brocade. But these items strained the Congressional budget for the first household. With the country at war, Lincoln did not ask for more money.

The décor suffered during the war years both from lack of funds and vandalism. Army troops were occasionally quartered in the East Room. During the these years, the mansion saw a lot of traffic. Carpeting was torn and drapes were snipped.

Mary Lincoln won no support for White House upkeep. As a Southerner, her motives were questioned at every turn. She was called a spendthrift and criticized for entertaining during a time of war.

The physical structure of the mansion changed little during the Civil War, but Lincoln did make one alteration. He arranged for a private passage on the second floor from the library through the reception room to his office. This allowed him to reach his private quarters without being seen by waiting strangers. Today this passage would go through the Yellow Oval Room and the Treaty Room, ending in the Lincoln Bedroom.

Andrew Johnson, the first President after the Civil War and one of only two ever impeached, still received money to redecorate the White House. In 1873, Grant also made large-scale decorative changes.

But by Grant's time, the White House began to look as if it would not survive. During this administration, one ceiling collapsed. All the rest were cracked. In the state rooms, they had settled several inches. The basement was damp, even unhealthy.

The commissioner of public buildings, assessing the situation, suggested that while the mansion, if "thoroughly repaired," could be used as an office, it was inadequate as a house. The private rooms numbered only eight. There were no closets in the bedrooms, and when large receptions were held, temporary bridges at the windows of the North Portico were necessary to aid people in leaving the building.

No major structural changes took place for a number of years despite these recommendations. Two large beams, supported by columns, were installed in the East Room during the Grant Administration. But the White House did see more redecorating. President Arthur, who won for himself the nickname "Elegant Arthur," was not pleased with the looks of the White House. He was in agreement with a visitor who described the mansion's furnishings as "modern abominations in upholstery and garish gilding." The rooms were called "staring, pretentious and Frenchy."

In 1882, Arthur auctioned off 24 wagonloads of White House merchandise to an eager crowd of about 5,000 persons. They grabbed up items such as hair mattresses, marble mantels, curtains, carpets, cuspidors, and a globe that had been the property of President Grant's daughter.

At right is the Red Room today, one of four state reception rooms in the White House.
At left is the Red Room in 1877—during the Rutherford B. Hayes Administration.

Louis C. Tiffany had the honor of putting the White House in order again. He redecorated the state rooms in a style that would become known as Art Nouveau. His famous stained-glass screen in the Entrance Hall had American eagles and flags "in the Arabian method."

Caroline Harrison, who with husband Benjamin occupied the Executive Mansion from 1889 to 1893, began a campaign to enlarge the aging building. With a family that included the Harrisons, her father, sister, a niece, a son and his wife and daughter, and another daughter and two infants, an enlargement seemed reasonable.

With Caroline's help, architect Fred D. Owen drew up three plans. One called for a separate residence to be located on 16th Street. A second called for minor additions to the existing structure.

The third plan was the most elaborate. It called for huge additions on each side of the White House. On the west side, there would be the "official wing" connected to the original building by corridors and a dome-shaped room filled with statues. On the east side, there would be the "historical art wing," similarly connected. On the south lawn, there was to be a huge conservatory filled with plants.

A circular palm house at each end would be shaped like the domed additions to the mansion.

On the south front of the mansion, a fountain was planned in honor of Christopher Columbus. Caroline hoped that the new building could be finished by Oct. 13, 1892, the centennial, or 100-year anniversary, of the White House.

But politics is an uncertain business, and Congress did not share the first lady's enthusiasm for the bill approving funds to build the new structures. She was not completely frustrated in her plans for the White House, however. Although she did not have her way with the exterior, she made a difference inside. There was a wholesale extermination of rats. Old, rotting floorboards were replaced, and the kitchen was modernized. Also, electric lights were installed.

One of Caroline's hobbies was painting china. Her interest led her to rummage around in an old china closet where pieces had been collecting since the beginning of the century. Eventually she began the White House China Collection, which is still in existence. It contains china from administrations beginning with George Washington.

The installation of electricity was important for two reasons. Not only did it allow the White House family to live in ever-increasing comfort, but it gave a young electrician, Ike Hoover, the opportunity to come to the White House for the first time. Hoover stayed and became the chief usher in the Executive Mansion for 42 years. His book, *Forty-Two Years in the White House,* gives invaluable information about how things looked and how life was lived in that institution for most of the first half of the 20th century. He writes: "In the kitchen of the original house … could be seen the old open fireplaces once used for broiling the chickens and baking the hoecakes for the early fathers of our country, the old cranes and spits still in place…. The west wing was hidden almost wholly by the old conservatory, where the couples would roam during parties and be lost among the tall palms and ferns!… There were bananas, oranges, lemons, figs and nuts of various kinds."

During the McKinley Administration from 1897 to 1901, there was still another call for enlarging the White House. The plan was for two rotundas—the east for offices, the west for more bedrooms. The original building would be used as a residence. This plan got no further than Caroline Harrison's earlier one.

Theodore Roosevelt Restoration

As the 20th century approached, the dream of an enlarged and improved White House came closer to realization. The feeling of the time was that not only should the White House be enlarged and structural problems remedied, but the building should be restored historically. The virtues of 18th-century décor, now far in the past, were becoming apparent.

Theodore Roosevelt called in the firm of McKim, Mead & White, which was well-known for its work with the "Colonial" style. In June 1902, Congressional appropriations came through. Work began immediately.

The architects found the ground floor in bad condition. Most of the second floor had settled dangerously. The sanitary system was in poor shape. Rainwater still drained through the walls via hollowed-out logs. Obsolete wiring and no adequate fire exits for servants' rooms in the attic made the possibility of fire real and frightening.

The firm reconstructed the interior and dug a new basement, where the heating system would be placed. The grounds at this time were still covered with greenhouses. In order to build the West Wing, these structures were torn down, revealing part of the foundations of Jefferson's 1807 west pavilion. These foundations were incorporated into the new west pavilion, which sheltered arriving visitors and led to the Executive Offices. At the same time, the east pavilion, torn down in 1869, was rebuilt.

When Charles McKim was finished with his decorating, the Victorian décor had disappeared. In its place was simple 18th-century elegance. The East Room, with parquet floors and no carpeting, took on the appearance it retains today. In the Entrance Hall, the Tiffany screen of Chester Arthur passed into history, as did his tile floors and the Benjamin Harrisons' ornamental frescoes. By late 19th-century standards, the rooms were plain, indeed. Gone were Julia Grant's Venetian glass vases decorated with boars' heads and President Arthur's chairs made of elk antlers.

Two cut-glass chandeliers made in London in 1790 light the Cross Hall.
At left is a portrait of President John F. Kennedy by Aaron Shikler.

The second floor became private quarters with construction of the West Wing, but living space was still small. Ellen Wilson made guest rooms in the attic in the 1910's.

When Calvin Coolidge became President in 1923, the Office of Public Parks and Buildings told him that the White House roof was about to fall in. Unruffled by the news, he replied that he "presumed there were plenty others who would be willing to take the risk" of residing under that roof. Still, in the spring and summer of 1927, the work of repairing the roof took place. At the same time, Hoban's third floor was added more than a century after the original architect had designed it. As a result, the Coolidges, who had moved out during construction and restoration, came home to a mansion with 18 new rooms.

Grace Coolidge took an active interest in the White House as an historic building. Thanks to her efforts, Congress passed a resolution that "rare old pieces" could be accepted as gifts to the White House. A committee was then appointed to evaluate these gifts for their quality and historic value. The committee was in existence through the Eisenhower years.

The Hoovers, who moved into the house in 1929, were both interested in White House history. Lou Hoover focused much of her attention on the Monroe period. She brought together the few pieces that were left from his time and put them in the room north of the upstairs Oval Room, which Elizabeth Monroe had used as a parlor. Lou also had some reproductions made from the furniture in Monroe's law office in nearby Fredericksburg, Va. From a storage area the Hoovers together rescued four chairs that were used by Lincoln and had them restored.

Although the Depression and the Second World War consumed most of the energy of the Franklin Roosevelts, there were some changes taking place at the White House during their long stay from 1933 to 1945. In 1934,

This cutaway view of the White House shows the interior of the ground floor and first floor. The South Portico appears in the foreground. When tours are available, the public may visit four state reception rooms and the State Dining Room on the first floor. The drawing also shows an exterior view of the second and third floors, which are not open for public viewing. The second floor contains the private living quarters of the President and the first family, as well as the Lincoln Bedroom, the Treaty Room, and the Queen's Room. The third floor contains guest rooms, staff quarters, and storage rooms.

Ground Floor

  1   Library
*2   Ground Floor Corridor
  3   Vermeil Room
  4   China Room
  5   Diplomatic Reception Room
  6   Map Room

First Floor

*7   East Room
*8   Green Room
*9   Blue Room
10   South Portico
*11 Red Room
*12 State Dining Room
13   Family Dining Room
*14 Cross Hall
*15 Entrance Hall

* Indicates areas open to the public when tours are available.

underground work space was added in the West Wing. A new East Wing was quickly put up during World War II. It supplied three stories of offices and a White House bomb shelter. F.D.R., who was a victim of polio, also needed special accommodations due to his disability. A swimming pool was built, and wheelchair ramps and elevators were installed.

Franklin Roosevelt's successor, Harry Truman, took an avid interest in White House architecture. When he built his famous Truman balcony in 1948 at a cost of $15,000, complaints were heard throughout the land. But Truman was unflinching. He said that he did not build it so that he would have a place to sun himself, but rather to break up the height of the giant 18th-century columns of the South Portico. Also, the balcony helped to shade the Blue Room.

After the Truman balcony was built, results of a $50,000 study Congress had appropriated showed that the White House was about to collapse in spite of the work that had been done earlier in the century. According to this study, only the outer walls were sound enough to be preserved. Interior walls had settled and cracked. The ancient wooden beams of 1817, which had been shot through with plumbing and wiring, were crumbling. The grand stairway was about to come down.

The White House seemed due for demolition. The idea of building a reproduction of the original building was introduced. Instead, the most complete restoration of the White House began in 1949.

Truman Restoration

Workers completely dismantled everything in the house, leaving only the outer walls. Furniture, chandeliers, mantelpieces, and decorative plaster were carted out and labeled. When the work was completed, the new White House had concrete underpinnings holding up the old walls, a new two-story basement, new foundations, and a steel frame. Décor was reinstalled. Inside, the mansion looked the same as before. One exception was that the main stairway had been moved so that it now descended into the Entrance Hall.

The Trumans moved back into the White House in March 1952. During the restoration they had lived in Blair House, across the street from the Executive Mansion. After the first

family returned, President Truman went on television to give America a tour of the restored house.

Before the 1949 restoration, there were no restrictions on how much the first family could alter the White House. Using Congressionally appropriated funds or their own money, new occupants could redecorate—even rebuild—as they wished. After the restoration the first family no longer had this prerogative.

During the Eisenhower Administration, there were no major changes in the mansion. In 1960, however, the Diplomatic Reception Room was redecorated in the style of the Federal period. In 1961, Jacqueline Kennedy made a major contribution to the White House as a national landmark and showplace for the nation. She formed the Fine Arts Committee for the White House and the Special Committee on Paintings. Her aim was to find authentic American antiques and paintings of the 18th and 19th centuries worthy of display at the White House. Also, in September 1961, Congress passed legislation that recognized the White House as a national museum. It stated that furniture of "historic interest" could become the "inalienable" property of the Executive Mansion, and that the Smithsonian Institution in Washington, D.C., would hold any object not in use.

Other first ladies had made contributions to the historical and artistic character of the White House. None, however, put the degree of effort into the task that Jacqueline Kennedy did.

She engaged Lorraine Pearce from the Smithsonian Institution to examine and catalogue items that were found in the mansion or brought there. Pieces included furniture, paintings, and other art objects.

One of the first finds at this time turned up in the broadcasting room in the White House itself. It was a heavily carved oak desk made from the wood of a British ship. It had been a present from Queen Victoria to President Rutherford B. Hayes in 1878. Every President from Hayes to Kennedy had used it, and Kennedy liked it so much, he put it in the Oval Office.

A central panel ordered by Franklin Roosevelt to hide his leg braces as he sat could swing open in the midfront of the desk. John Kennedy, Jr., who called the large desk "my house," used the central panel as his "secret door" while playing in the office.

Other highlights in the search of items of interest during the Kennedy Administration included a sofa that had once been the property of Dolley Madison, a chair ordered from Paris by President Monroe in 1817, and a mirror used by George Washington.

In February 1962, Jacqueline Kennedy went on television, much as President Truman had done in 1952. Acting as a tour guide for the nation, she took her audience into the public rooms. Some were completed, and others were still being restored. She was praised for her command of history, one of her favorite areas of interest.

The result of Jacqueline's work was that many more tourists poured into the Executive Mansion after the broadcast than had come before. She was also responsible for initiating the publication of *The White House, An Historic Guide,* which aids visitors in understanding the significance of the mansion.

Since the Kennedy term, others have continued the work of finding appropriate art objects for display in the White House. Many First Ladies have taken a special interest in the history of the White House. Pat Nixon added 18 portraits of Presidents and First Ladies. Rosalynn Carter added 24 major works to the permanent collection of American paintings. Hillary Clinton initiated eight exhibitions of 1900's American sculpture.

Our National Museum

One of the exciting things about the White House is that it shows the nation's growth and change, reflecting many periods and décors. The mansion has undergone three major restorations in the 20th century. Each has contributed to its historic importance.

Today's White House has 132 rooms, both public and private, and beautiful gardens on its landscaped grounds. Discussing them all would be quite a task. Due to their historic and cultural significance, however, the East Room, Blue Room, Red Room, Green Room, Lincoln Sitting Room, Cross and Entrance Halls, China

George Healy's portrait of Lincoln hangs in the State Dining Room. Inscribed in the mantel below is John Adams' White House Prayer.

Room, Oval Office, Rose Garden, Garden Room, and Jacqueline Kennedy Garden are among the most outstanding.

The White House leans heavily on 18th and early 19th century styles. The elegant East Room, called the "Public Audience Room" by its creator James Hoban, is the largest and most formal of the state reception rooms. Its fame began humbly when Abigail Adams had the household laundry hung within its still-barren walls. Dolley Madison did likewise.

Since the East Room was completed in 1829, it has had a more distinguished history. Its classical décor dates largely from the 1902 renovation of Theodore Roosevelt. Fontainebleau parquetry was installed as well as upholstered benches and three Bohemian cut glass chandeliers. The walls, paneled in wood and featuring delicate carving, were painted white. Plaster decoration adorns the ceiling.

Gold and white had been the original choice for draperies during the 1902 renovation, although the architect preferred red. During the Franklin Roosevelt Administration, red draperies were hung. The switch was made back to gold and white during the Truman renovation. New marble mantels were also installed over the four fireplaces. In the early 1960's, the mantels were painted off-white to match the walls. In 1965, gold damask draperies from France were hung. Gilbert Stuart's 1796 portrait of George Washington is in this room.

The East Room has seen more than its share of history, both in national tragedy and celebration. Seven Presidents have lain in state here. Large gatherings such as the weddings of three Presidents' daughters—Nellie Grant, Alice Roosevelt, and Lynda Johnson—have also taken place here.

Other events the East Room has become known for include White House entertainments. It was in the East Room that renowned cellist Pablo Casals gave a concert in 1961, during Kennedy's Administration.

President Monroe chose the furniture for the Blue and Red rooms in the Empire style, which was in vogue during his Administration. He thought the style reflected favorably upon the dignity of the nation.

The Blue Room is in the French Empire style. Oval, it was known early on as the "elliptic saloon," or salon. Central to the Blue Room's collection are eight pieces of the original furnishings, including a bergeré—an armchair with enclosed sides—and a gilded bronze clock.

It was President Van Buren who first coined the phrase "Blue Room" in 1837. President Buchanan sold Monroe's furniture in 1860. He replaced it with then-more-fashionable Victorian rococo-revival furniture, which lasted until the renovation in Theodore Roosevelt's time. McKim, Mead & White designed furniture based on the original. The floor became parquet and the walls were covered with blue silk.

The Blue Room contains a number of paintings that have become familiar to many generations of Americans. Their reproductions hang in schoolrooms and appear in textbooks. In the Blue Room, one will meet Presidents John Adams, Thomas Jefferson, John Tyler, Andrew Jackson, and the Monroes—Elizabeth and James.

The Blue Room was renovated and refurbished in the early 1990's. The project was completed in mid-1995. The blue fabric used for the draperies and furniture is similar to that which decorated the room in the 1800's. The upholstery fabric retains the gold eagle medallion on the chair backs, which was adapted from a Monroe-era chair depicted in a portrait of Monroe. A new oval carpet, based on the design of the carpet acquired for the room by President Monroe in 1815, completed the renovation project.

The Red Room is another of the four state reception rooms in the White House. In the 19th century, it was used as a music room, where families gathered on Sunday evenings. Occasionally included among the furnishings have been musical instruments such as a pianoforte and guitar ordered by Dolley Madison.

The Red Room was refurbished in 2000. The furniture dates from about 1810 to 1830. Done in the style called American Empire, it resembles the French Empire furniture in the Blue Room. Featured is the work of French-born cabinetmaker Charles Honoré Lannuier.

The Red Room was known as the Washington Parlor during the Polk and Tyler administrations. Then it contained the famous Gilbert Stuart portrait of George Washington.

In the latter half of the 19th century, the Red Room was filled with many Victorian furnishings. During the 1902 renovation, they were removed. Also, most of the collection of first lady portraits that had been there at the end of the 19th century were relocated to the ground floor corridor. The only exception is the portrait of Dolley Madison, which hangs on the north wall.

The Green Room, a drawing room, was completely refurbished in 1971. It is in the style

The Blue Room is decorated in the original French Empire style.

of the Federal period, 1800 to 1815. The eagle, a favorite decorative motif during this period, is found in several places. With wings outspread, it stands on ornamental cornices at the windows and at the top of the mirror above the fireplace mantel, for example.

The Green Room had a green color scheme as early as the Jefferson Administration. John Quincy Adams called it the "Green Drawing Room" when he was President.

The use of the room varied in the early 1800's. At first, under John Adams, it was a "lodging room." Jefferson used it as a drawing room, Madison as a sitting room, Monroe as a room for playing cards with guests and relaxing informally. John Quincy Adams used it as a drawing room, for small teas and receptions. Sometimes, formal dinners were held there. It has been used as a drawing room ever since.

The Green Room's furniture is in the style of Duncan Phyfe, a noted American furniture maker of the late 1700's and early 1800's. During Coolidge's term, original pieces of Federal-period furniture were chosen for this room.

Paintings in the Green Room include portraits of Benjamin Franklin, John Quincy

Adams, his wife Louisa, James Madison, James Monroe, Rutherford B. Hayes, and Benjamin Harrison. Franklin's portrait, painted in 1767 from life by David Martin, is considered among the finest portraits in the White House collection.

The Lincoln Sitting Room is furnished in the late Empire and Victorian styles. Little-used until 1825, the room became a busy office for the President and his staff in the 1860's. In 1902, it became part of the family quarters when the West Wing of the White House was built.

The Lincoln Sitting Room was last redecorated during the Kennedy Administration. The four rosewood chairs date from about 1860 and were probably bought by Mary Todd Lincoln. Although most of the furniture in the room is Victorian, a small desk made by James Hoban sits in front of the south window. The green-and-yellow print fabric on the walls was copied from a 19th-century pattern. The curtains are a quaint paisley. In addition to the many mementos of the Lincoln period in this room are early drawings of Pierre L'Enfant's plan for the District of Columbia and 19th-century prints that show how the city grew.

The Cross and Entrance Halls were at the center of James Hoban's original design of the White House, and they have not changed substantially over the years. However, modifications have been made to the design and placement of the main staircases. The Cross Hall connects all of the state rooms and opens into the Entrance Hall, which is a large reception area.

During the 1800's, two staircases led to the second floor. During the 1902 renovation, the staircase at the west end of the Cross Hall was removed to increase the size of the State Dining Room. At the same time, the second staircase was enlarged. During the 1848-1852 renovation, this staircase was moved to open into the Entrance Hall. It is now referred to as the Grand Staircase. An English cut-glass chandelier from about 1810 to 1815 lights the staircase at the first landing. Today, the Grand Staircase is often used on ceremonial occasions.

The Cross Hall has marble walls and floors, which were added during the Truman renovation. The hall is lighted by two Adam-style cut-glass chandeliers. The bronze light standards were added during the 1902 renovation.

The Entrance Hall is set off from the Cross Hall by a colonnade and is decorated in the same style. Furnishings in the Entrance Hall include a French pier table purchased by President Monroe and a pair of French settees with carved mahog-any swan heads. In 1973, a suite of 1800's Italian gilded furniture of the Empire style was placed in the Cross and Entrance Halls.

Paintings of Presidents of the 1900's hang along the Grand Staircase, including Harry S. Truman by Greta Kempton, Dwight D. Eisenhower and Richard Nixon by J. Anthony Wills, Herbert J. Hoover by Elmer W. Greene, and Warren Harding by F. Luis Mora. Portraits of recent Presidents hang in the Cross and Entrance Halls, including John F. Kennedy by Aaron Shikler, Lyndon Johnson by Elizabeth Shoumatoff, Gerald Ford by Everett Raymond Kinstler, and Jimmy Carter by Herbert E. Abrams.

Kennedy hosts a concert by cellist
Pablo Casals in the East Room, 1961.

The China Collection, first started by Caroline Harrison, is housed in the China Room. Ida Saxton McKinley and Edith Roosevelt continued her work and expanded the collection greatly. Caroline also started the practice of breaking damaged china and dumping it in the Potomac rather than giving it away or selling it.

Not every President orders new china, and Presidents have traditionally taken their china with them when they leave office. Much of the collection now in the White House was bought from the descendants of first families or at auctions. The Lyndon Johnson china was given to the White House in 1968.

The China Room has little furniture in it. The china is displayed in red-velvet-lined cabinets contrasting with off-white walls. The color red is picked up again in the Indo-Ispahan rug, which was handwoven in about 1850. It has a circular, flowered pattern. Also of great prominence in the room, and the item around which the color scheme was built, is a stunning portrait of the fashionable Grace Coolidge, who posed in a long red dress with her dog at the side.

White House Gardens

From the Oval Office, the President can look out on the famous Rose Garden. Here many presidential receptions are held. Foreign dignitaries, Medal of Honor recipients, U.S. astronauts, even the 1972 table tennis delegation from the People's Republic of China have all been received here. Queen Elizabeth II of the United Kingdom was the guest of honor at a state dinner in the garden when she visited during the Bicentennial celebration. In 1971, the Rose Garden was the scene of the wedding of Tricia Nixon to Edward Cox.

From the beginning of White House history, this area was designated as a garden. A diary of the early 1800's recorded, "After breakfast we walked . . . to the ground behind the President's House, which [will be] enclosed and laid out for a garden. It is at present in great confusion, having on it old brick kilns [and] pits to contain water used by the brick makers."

Ellen Wilson first planted roses here in 1913. In 1962, President Kennedy requested that the garden be redesigned.

The Garden Room in the East Wing looks out on the Jacqueline Kennedy Garden, named in honor of the first lady by her successor, Lady Bird Johnson. It contains flowering trees, shrubs, and flower beds and provides a lovely setting for informal receptions given by first ladies. Alongside the garden is a colonnade, built in 1902. It is true to the original design as approved by Jefferson.

The Garden Room is decorated in the Regency style. An English style of furniture of the early 19th century, it incorporates Oriental elements. The yellow lacquered chairs, for example, are carved to look like bamboo.

Apart from the formal gardens, some landscaping is associated with specific Presidents. There are, for example, the American elm of John Quincy Adams, the magnolia planted by Andrew Jackson, and the giant sequoia, associated with Richard Nixon.

From time to time, tours of the White House are suspended for security reasons. When tours are held, they begin at the East Wing. Visitors may see only five public rooms on the first floor: The East Room, the Blue Room, the Red Room, the Green Room, and the State Dining Room. In 1995, the National Park Service opened the White House Visitor Center. Located two blocks east of the White House, at 1450 Pennsylvania Avenue, the facility distributes White House public tour tickets, maintains educational exhibits, and houses an information desk and the White House Historical Association gift shop.

Private White House

The private rooms at the White House are used every day by the First Family, their guests, and the President's staff. On the first floor, the Family Dining Room is used for official occasions involving a small number of guests. The furniture is in the styles of the Federal period.

The ground floor also contains private rooms. The kitchen is here, plus the offices of the White House physician and curator. The Diplomatic Reception Room serves as an entrance to the White House for the family and ambassadors. The wallpaper shows American landscapes from the first half of the 1800's. The Library, which contained "tubs, buckets, and a variety of lumber" in 1801, now has works that span American thought and tradition. The Map Room was used during World War II as a situation room. Now a private meeting room, it contains Chippendale furniture. The Vermeil Room, sometimes called the Gold Room, serves as a display room and for formal occasions, as a ladies sitting room. Vermeil, or gilded silver, pieces are featured in this room.

Private living quarters on the second floor include the Lincoln Bedroom, the Treaty Room, and the Queen's Suite. The Lincoln Bedroom is a guest room containing furniture from the Lincoln era—American Victorian furnishings from 1850 to 1870. Lincoln used this room as an office and Cabinet Room. The Lincoln Suite includes the bedroom and the Lincoln Sitting Room.

The Treaty Room served as the Cabinet room for 10 administrations, from Andrew Johnson through Theodore Roosevelt. The room's name was chosen during the Kennedy Administration to show the many important decisions made there. Normally used as a private meeting room, the Treaty Room has also been used for signing several important documents. The room has Victorian furnishings that resemble those of the Cabinet Room during the Grant Administration. Facsimiles of U.S. treaties hang in the Treaty Room.

The Queen's Bedroom and a small sitting room make up the Queen's Suite, which is furnished in the styles of the American Federal period. Many royal guests have stayed here. Decorated today in shades of rose and white, this room was once used by the Presidents' staff. It was also used as an emergency telegraph office when President Garfield languished after being fatally shot by an assassin.

The third floor of the White House is also set aside for private living quarters.

The White House Lifestyle

While in the White House, members of the first family are both honored guests and public servants. Although afforded many luxuries, the demands placed on them are endless, particularly with regard to the President and the first lady.

President George Washington saw the presidency as a sort of divine burden. Presidents often suffer under the weight of the task. Although they are surrounded by beauty and elegance, they have little time to stroll in the Rose Garden or relax on a quiet evening in the luxury of the Yellow Oval Room.

Today's President can never escape from the job. Reports may be read in the evening, and the President's sleep may be broken by a sudden emergency either in the United States or in a foreign land. Even when the President travels, the White House mail pouch arrives each day with papers to read and sign.

The President's workday has varied, however. Chester A. Arthur was able to put in only four-day weeks. He also took three hours off for lunch. The day began for him at 10 a.m.

Franklin Roosevelt rose early, had breakfast in bed, and looked at the major newspapers before leaving for his office in the West Wing of the White House. He seemed to enjoy his work and often worked late into the night.

John F. Kennedy's morning routine was much like F.D.R.'s. He began at about 7:30 a.m. When he awoke, he was immediately alert and began reading the morning papers before he got out of bed. Within 15 minutes, he could read four newspapers, absorbing all the important details. It was said that he continually caught staff members off guard with comments about newspaper stories they had missed.

Presidents usually put in a long work week that revolves around a series of meetings and appointments. Many are with staff from the executive branch, including the Cabinet meetings, over which the President presides. Legislative leaders and the press also meet with the chief executive.

Beforehand, members of the White House staff brief the President on the topics that will be discussed. Daily briefings from the director of the Central Intelligence Agency and the assistant for national security affairs keep the President up to date on security matters.

The President sees many visitors other than Washington government personnel. These include labor leaders, political workers, civic leaders from around the nation, and representatives from youth groups. President Truman received visitors from 10 or 11 A.M. to 1 P.M.,

and again from 3 P.M. to 4 P.M. or longer. In a typical day, Eisenhower had 15 appointments during which he saw perhaps 40 persons.

The Kennedy appointment schedule was full and tight. For example, the appointments secretary might have scheduled himself in from 9:17 to 9:20 A.M. and someone else from 9:20 to 9:30 A.M. Appointments went on like this all day with no letup.

Weather permitting, visitors may meet the President briefly in the Rose Garden of the White House. To save time, visitors must give the appointments secretary a memorandum of subjects to be discussed long before the meeting. The President receives this memorandum just before the conference.

The President's social duties take up much time. As chief of state, the President gives official dinners at the White House for the diplomatic corps, the Supreme Court, and the Vice-President. Presidents hold a half-dozen formal receptions a year, as well as special dinners and receptions for dignitaries.

Susan Ford, daughter of President Gerald Ford, held her senior prom at the White House.

The most frequent entertainers among the Presidents are said to have been Martin Van Buren and Chester A. Arthur. Theodore Roosevelt was fond of lively luncheon conversations and tried to have three or four guests of varying background to keep discussion interesting.

Franklin and Eleanor Roosevelt shared a love for White House living. Perhaps more than any other First Couple, they regarded the White House as their home and enjoyed their long stay there.

The White House was not new to the Roosevelts. Both were related to "Uncle Ted" Roosevelt, who gave Eleanor away at their wedding. As a young man, Franklin had been a guest at the White House. He had eaten at the presidential dinner table and slept in the family's private quarters.

Franklin and Eleanor loved to entertain. Eleanor enjoyed being with the public and could shake hands all afternoon and again that evening with Franklin. Thousands of guests attended buffets, dinners, and receptions at the White House during the F.D.R. Administration.

The Roosevelts received many dignitaries from foreign lands. In honor of a visit from the king and queen of England, George VI and Elizabeth, in 1939, rooms in the private quarters were refurbished.

Other foreign dignitaries who visited the Roosevelts included Foreign Minister Molotov of the Soviet Union; George II, King of Greece; Peter II of Yugoslavia; Queen Wilhelmina of Holland; and Madame Chiang Kai-shek of China. To sustain him during his stay, Molotov brought black bread, sausages, and a pistol.

It was Franklin Roosevelt who established Camp David as a retreat in 1942. It is in a heavily wooded area of Catoctin Mountain in Maryland, about 70 miles (113 kilometers) from the capital. It covers about 200 acres (81 hectares). Roosevelt used the camp to escape the summer heat in Washington.

In 1945, Harry Truman made the camp, then called Shangri-la, the official presidential retreat. Dwight Eisenhower renamed it in 1953 for his grandson, David Eisenhower. He also added a golf course. The camp has a swimming pool and other sports facilities.

The Eisenhowers also enjoyed their stay at the White House but for their own reasons. An army couple, they had traveled all their lives and had known long separations. They enjoyed having a permanent home in the White House for eight years. Said Ike, "At last I've got a job where I can stay home nights, and by golly, I'm going to stay home."

The Eisenhowers entertained their share of eminent guests from abroad. Visiting the Eisenhower White House were his wartime colleague Winston Churchill; the young queen of England, Elizabeth; and King Saud of Saudi Arabia.

The Kennedy Administration saw a youthful White House with fresh ideas and a concern for the arts and gracious living. The Kennedys entertained lavishly. Like Thomas Jefferson, they employed a French chef to prepare state dinners, which they shortened to four courses. That left time to present performances such as Shakespearean plays and classical music concerts, of which the Casals concert was one. There was also dancing in the East Room.

For relaxation, Presidents have turned to various forms of entertainment. Grover Cleveland and Herbert Hoover liked fishing. Eisenhower also did, but he had other hobbies including outdoor cooking, bridge, and golf—for which he was most known. In 1954, Eisenhower installed a putting green on the White House lawn so that he could practice his shots. In the 1950's, golf became a national passion.

Theodore Roosevelt had many interests. For example, he liked to box, hike, and hunt. Franklin Roosevelt collected stamps and swam. Kennedy also enjoyed swimming and used the White House pool before lunch and in the evening to keep in shape and release tension. On the wall of the pool room during the New Englander's term was painted a Massachusetts waterfront scene, a token of the Kennedy family's love of the sea.

George H.W. Bush installed horseshoe pits and a tennis court in 1989. Two years later, he added a basketball court. The small outdoor court proved insufficient for Barack Obama. Shortly after taking office, he had the tennis court adapted so that it could accommodate a full court game of basketball.

Busy First Ladies

The responsibility for planning and overseeing White House social functions falls on the first lady. In cases where a President has no wife—such as Jefferson, Buchanan, and Cleveland, at first—whoever the President selects as official hostess takes on these duties. The first lady today supervises a large social as well as domestic staff, and she has her own office and secretarial help.

Some first ladies have been involved in gov-

Eleanor Roosevelt visits troops in the South Pacific as a representative of the American Red Cross in 1943.

ernmental activities. Nellie Herron Taft, for example, was a driving force behind her husband's political career. Even though she suffered a stroke two months after the inauguration, she soon continued to sit in on staff and other meetings her husband held. Woodrow Wilson had a stroke in 1919, which left him nearly incapacitated. For the remainder of his time in office, Edith, whom Wilson had married as a widower in 1915, handled day-to-day details of government.

Eleanor Roosevelt traveled extensively for the handicapped President in the 1930's. Franklin's "eyes and ears," she was soon as well known as he, and personally Eleanor was known to many more people. She wrote a daily newspaper column, held frequent press conferences, and gave lectures. During World War II, she visited troops in various theaters of war.

Pat Nixon and Jacqueline Kennedy traveled widely too, on numerous good-will missions to other countries. Lady Bird Johnson's major interest lay in beautifying the capital with gardens and flowers and in Head Start programs for preschool children. Mental health projects occupied Rosalynn Carter as honorary head of the President's commission on that topic. Nancy Reagan was active in the fight against drug abuse by young people. Barbara Bush worked to promote family reading and literacy programs.

Hillary Rodham Clinton, an influential attorney, served as the head of a task force on health care reform during her husband's Administration. Mrs. Clinton later served as a senator from New York and as U.S. secretary of state. In 2016, she became the first female major party nominee for president, but she lost the general election to Republican Donald Trump.

As a former public school librarian, Laura Bush turned her passion for books into a campaign for promoting reading, education, and teaching. Michelle Obama has spoken out on issues that affect military families. She also helped lead a nationwide campaign to fight childhood obesity.

Dining with the Presidents

Beginning in Washington's day, the presidential mansion has been the center of capital society. White House gatherings are often splendid affairs and food and refreshments are plentiful.

Thomas Jefferson was the least formal of Presidents. While stressing gracious simplicity in style and manner, Jefferson set a sumptuous gourmet table from 1801 to 1809. He frequently accompanied his steward, Etienne Lemaine, to the Georgetown market in Washington, seeking out crabs, oysters, and other seafood, plus olives, various fruits, and choice cuts of meat. It was said that Jefferson spent an average of $50 a day on food purchases, and that his wine bill during his two terms in office ran to around $10,000. All this, plus other expenses, came out of Jefferson's $25,000 salary or pocket.

Desserts interested Jefferson. He brought back a recipe for ice cream when minister to France after the French Revolution, and he is credited with popularizing the dish in the White House. It frequently serves as one of the White House desserts.

Jefferson also liked persimmon beer. His recipe called for 8 bushels of persimmons, crushed and kneaded. This was mixed with bran and baked into loaves, then crumbled into a powder and covered with 40 gallons (151 liters) of water for two to three days. Finally, the water was drawn off, boiled, and hops were added, along with more water. This mixture was then allowed to ferment.

The Fabulous Dolley

Of all White House hostesses, Dolley Madison is probably the most famous. She served sometimes as hostess for widower Thomas Jefferson while her husband James was secretary of state. From 1809 to 1817, she was first lady of the mansion.

Dolley was a thoughtful hostess. She brought out refreshments even to those visiting the White House for a brief time. She has been credited with introducing the practice of serving bouillon at afternoon receptions on cold days. A batch of Dolley's bouillon was made from 4 pounds (1.8 kilograms) of beef and a portion of veal, along with turnips, carrots, red pepper, onions, salt, and 6 quarts (5.7 liters) of water. The ingredients simmered for 6 hours. After standing overnight, the bouillon was

reheated with a touch of sherry. Four-layer cake was another Dolley Madison specialty.

From 1825 to 1829, the guests of dour John Quincy Adams needed invitations to be admitted to gatherings. Servants served refreshments such as ice lemonade, port wine, small cakes, and, of course, ice cream.

James Buchanan, President from 1857 to 1861, possessed gourmet tastes like Jefferson. Buchanan often employed a caterer to provide food for receptions and dinners, a service that excelled in lobsters, oysters, terrapin, wild turkey, and partridge. Harriet Lane, Buchanan's niece and hostess, was usually hard-pressed to keep food budgets within any sort of limit.

On May 21, 1874, when Ulysses and Julia Grant's daughter Nellie married, the wedding breakfast in the State Dining Room offered fare much different from what the general had known in the army. It included soft-shelled crabs on toast, chicken croquettes with fresh peas, aspic of beef tongue, and boiled spring chicken. Strawberries with cream, ice cream, cakes, punch, coffee, and chocolate concluded the meal.

Grover Cleveland's wedding to Frances Folsom took place in the Blue Room at 7 p.m. on June 2, 1886. In the Family Dining Room, the centerpiece on the table for the informal supper afterward was a ship made of roses and pansies. It rested on a mirror representing a lake. The meal was terrapin, spring chicken, cold meats, salads, a variety of fish, paté de foie gras, ice cream, bonbons, and fruits.

Royalty have dined well at the White House. The most lavish entertainment of this type came with the visit of the king and queen of England to the Franklin Roosevelts. A luncheon featured cantaloupe balls, green turtle soup, and broiled sweetbread. Mushrooms, asparagus, and salad completed the relatively simple menu.

In the evening, the dinner in the State Dining Room stood in contrast. There, 82 people gathered at a U-shaped table to enjoy clam cocktail, calf's head soup, broiled filet of flounder, mushroom and wine sauce, sliced tomatoes, and boned capon. Also presented were cranberry sauce, peas, buttered beets, sweet potato puffs, and frozen cheese and cress salad. Dessert was maple and almond ice cream.

The next day saw a return of simplicity and a change of scene. At the Roosevelts' estate at Hyde Park, N.Y., Eleanor served the king and queen hot dogs, to the chagrin of some critical observers.

Queen Elizabeth II of the United Kingdom addresses guests at a state dinner at the White House in 2007.

The Clintons shunned traditional French cuisine served by previous administrations in favor of an all-American theme for their first official dinner at the White House. Even the entertainment was all-American: the dinner was preceded by the Super Bowl and followed by a concert at which Broadway performers sang songs about nearly every state.

For George W. and Laura Bush's first state dinner, they played host to Mexican President Vicente Fox and his wife, Martha Sahagun de Fox. When Bush's father hosted a Mexican president at the White House, an international incident was narrowly avoided by the quick-thinking social secretary. The pastry chef had constructed an adobe house of edible sweets, which included a little candy Mexican boy taking a siesta with a sombrero over his eyes. It was this image of his people that the Mexican president was trying to erase. Just as the platter was being carried from the kitchen to the State Dining Room, the President's social secretary noticed the sweet sleeping boy and plucked it from the dessert.

This time around, the second Bush to live in the White House served Maryland crab and chorizo pozole with summer vegetables; pumpkin seed-crusted bison with whipped potato, fava bean, and chanterelle ragout and apple chipotle sauce; salads of gold and red tomatoes and greens; followed by mango and coconut ice cream served with peaches, raspberries, red chili pepper sauce, and tequila sabayon.

As the White House continues to serve as "home" to America's President, the nation has cause to reflect. Much has changed, but much has also remained the same. Americans still hotly argue anything that issues from the White House, from critical foreign and domestic policy decisions to the details of presidential protocol, dress, and dining. Serious journalists find the time to discuss whether the President should buy new china, and everyday citizens make their feelings known about how to deal with terrorism.

The opinions of Americans have been heard behind the walls of the manor along the Potomac for many decades. There has been much change within, but they still stand, just as the President of a free people still listens.

Washington:
The President's Hometown

Throughout Washington, D.C., gleaming federal buildings and memorials wrapped in rich green splendor beckon visitors to marvel at the monumental reality of the U.S. government. For this alabaster city is where government makes and preserves the laws of the land. And this is where the President lives.

An estimated 20 million people come to Washington, D.C., each year. Some come to conduct business with the government. Most others come as tourists to see Congress in session and to visit the White House, the Capitol, and other government buildings and historic sites.

Washington's business is government. Most cities have a combination of commerce, industry, government, and agricultural ventures to bolster their economy. However, the federal government is Washington's primary employer. Because of its concentration of government services, Washington has frequently been called "Uncle Sam's Company Town." It is one of the few cities in the world built solely to administer government.

Washington provides a curious blend of power, politics, and culture. Tourists may stare at the sight of a presidential motorcade or members of Congress rushing across the Capitol plaza. But to Washingtonians, mingling with public figures and tourists, for that matter, is part of living in Washington.

Many residents have lived in the capital a short time and will probably move on soon. New government employees arrive with each administration. Capital dwellers come from every state and scores of countries. This produces a cosmopolitan atmosphere. The city belongs to all groups without any one sector dominating.

As a planned city, Washington molded its own personality. With laws prohibiting structures over 160 feet (49 meters) high and putting pollution limits on industry, Washington protects its past while ensuring its future.

Guidance from each President has added a personal flavor to the national capital. Presidents have had trees planted, urged improvements, and made Washington a city of hospitality. History is carefully preserved there. A stroll through the city's broad streets can trigger memories of many big events in U.S. history.

Page 104: Washington, D.C., lures visitors to its white magnificence.

In its infancy, the U.S. government met in several cities before choosing the Potomac River as the site for the nation's capital. Various locations were necessary during the Revolutionary War to protect the Continental Congress from advancing British troops. After the war, many states wanted the government seat located within their borders, and this kept lawmakers moving.

The need for a single capital had already become evident by 1783, when several hundred angry soldiers seeking back pay for their services marched on Congress in Philadelphia, Pa. Neither state nor local governments offered to protect members of Congress, who could not maintain their own defense.

New York Capital

When George Washington became the first President of the United States in 1789, he took the oath of office in New York City, the first capital under the Constitution. At the time, the city boasted a population of about 30,000, including many slaves. The city had a rich social life, equally varied business and industry, and all the conveniences to create a stirring inauguration.

Throngs of visitors poured into New York City to see the new President. Taverns and boarding houses overflowed, so many people pitched tents in city streets to await the festivities. Meanwhile, Major Pierre Charles L'Enfant, a French architect who would later design Washington, D.C., remodeled the original 1699 New York City Hall into Federal Hall. For the President's first residence, an elegant house on Cherry Street was rented. He moved to yet another rented home during his stay in New York.

After Washington took his oath of office on the balcony of Federal Hall, a flag was raised, guns fired, and church bells rang. Washington then gave his inaugural address to an entourage that accompanied him to St. Paul's Chapel for a special service—a tradition of inaugural prayer that has been revived by recent Presidents.

By the time New York state voted to commission the building of an official residence for the President, a move was under way to find a new site for the capital. The Constitution provided for a city unhampered by state and local tensions, but the exact location was left to Congress.

An early map of the City of Washington shows rectangular blocks cut by major avenues that meet in circles.

New York City's steamy summers and cold winters only fanned the jealousies that were smoldering among the states. Several laid claim to the nation's capital. Both the North and the South wanted the capital in their region.

The dispute dragged on. Citizens popularized the theme in poems and songs. According to one ditty:

> Oh what a charming thing and pretty
> To have a noble Federal City.
> Then let us to the woods repair
> And build a Federal City there.

On July 16, 1790, Northerners and Southerners traded votes on two bills that finally settled the controversy. Secretary of the Treasury Alexander Hamilton wanted Congress to repay state war debts so the country could establish credit at home and abroad. Southerners opposed Hamilton's plan. About the same time, Secretary of State Thomas Jefferson expressed his preference for a Southern capital on the Potomac River. Hamilton and Jefferson worked out an agreement. The federal government assumed responsibility for all state war debts in exchange for the nation's capital being built on land donated by the Southern States of Maryland and Virginia. Compromise also determined that Philadelphia would be Congress's home for the next 10 years until a permanent capital could be built along the Potomac.

Philadelphia was the second largest and perhaps the most cosmopolitan city of the day, drawing its approximately 28,500 residents from all elements of the U.S. population. Since it had been the seat of government in the past, it easily adapted to being national headquarters. With varied businesses such as shipping, tanning, and metalworking, the city was affected little by the affairs of government. As political logrolling and gossiping blossomed, everyday activities continued. It was an exciting city.

High living costs, however, disturbed many officials. George Washington found it difficult to maintain a household within the limits of his $25,000 salary and entertain in the manner expected of a President.

Washington examined many areas along the Potomac before selecting an area 10 miles (16 kilometers) square for the new federal district. The tract of land incorporated part of Maryland, including George Town (later Georgetown), and an area from Virginia, including Alexandria. Georgetown and Alexandria were to retain their local governments, while two smaller settlements, Carrollsburg and Hamburg, were absorbed by the Federal City.

A Port at the Potomac?

Since he already owned land in Alexandria, Washington knew the commercial and industrial possibilities of this rolling swamp and forest. He thought a port at the Potomac would become a great commercial center with access north, south, and west. The Federal City would express all the strength of the new nation.

As one of the first steps in carrying out his great plan, Washington sent Andrew Ellicott, a surveyor noted for setting parts of the New York and Pennsylvania state borders, to survey the area and fix boundaries. Locating and supervising the construction of public buildings was assigned to three commissioners— Daniel Carroll, Thomas Johnson, and David Stuart.

Large portions of land were to be donated by Maryland and Virginia. The two states added $120,000 and $72,000, respectively, to be used to erect government buildings. Additional revenue was to come from land sales within the area.

Private landowners were approached to sell their property. Some were more reluctant to sell than others. Washington accompanied his commissioners to negotiate a plan whereby owners would contribute some parcels of their land for public use and sell others. To deter speculation in areas that were expected to hold government buildings, he ordered surveys in different locations to keep sellers guessing.

According to a March 30, 1791, agreement, 19 original owners sold their property for about $65 per acre ($26 per hectare) and donated extra land for streets and avenues.

At first, landowners were satisfied because the price was more than the land was worth for farming. Then they heard about the proposed architectural scheme that allowed for expansive avenues up to 160 feet (49 meters) wide.

That meant almost half their acreage was being contributed for streets.

The innovative designer responsible for this unusual arrangement was Major Pierre L'Enfant, the French architect and engineer. He had been an eager volunteer in the American Revolution. L'Enfant wanted the opportunity now to build a monumental city filled with grand public buildings, broad landscaped avenues, and open spaces.

L'Enfant had heard gossip about Congressional plans for the Federal City and asked President Washington in 1789 for the honor of creating a magnificent capital. Since Washington knew L'Enfant's ability as a professional military engineer and respected his creative talents, L'Enfant was appointed to draw up a plan for the Federal City. His assistants were Andrew Ellicott, who was named chief surveyor, and Benjamin Banneker, a self-educated, free black mathematician and surveyor. Working with them, L'Enfant began the layout for what has remained the essence of Washington, D.C., since that time. They followed an idea that Thomas Jefferson had given L'Enfant. It called for a diamond-shaped capital.

In 1791, the three commissioners announced that the city would be named the city of Washington in honor of the President. President Washington continued to call the project the "Federal City."

Together, Washington and L'Enfant decided on Jenkins Hill, the highest point in the city, as the site for the "Congress House," or the Capitol. It was to be about 1 mile (1.6 kilometers) from the President's House, a structure L'Enfant imagined to be patterned after the French palace of Versailles. This distance was considered to be far enough to require formal transportation of anyone delivering a message, yet close enough for the President to be aware of all workings of government.

Where today's Mall is located, L'Enfant recommended a 400-foot- (122-meter-) wide public walk. The broad sweep of walkway went from the Capitol due west to the Potomac, then a right-angle turn led to the President's House.

As these early decisions were made, the next logical scheme was to add a street connecting the two major buildings. This "grand esplanade" was called Pennsylvania Avenue. A large area north of the avenue was reserved for a central market. Plans for statues, including one sculpture of George Washington to stand where the Washington Monument was later built, a national church, fountains, and elaborate monuments bespeckled the architect's layout.

As his dream unfolded, L'Enfant's basic distrust of business people made compromise difficult. He was so sure they would ruin his grand scheme by making speculative land deals that he refused to reproduce his survey map for the commissioners who were still negotiating land sales.

Because copies were unavailable, a house was discovered under construction where he had proposed New Jersey Avenue. When L'Enfant ordered the house removed, its owner, Daniel Carroll, an influential nephew of the commissioner, refused. L'Enfant responded by trying to tear down the house himself.

Repeated confrontations with the stubborn architect eventually led to his dismissal. L'Enfant then charged the government about $95,000 for his services. Congress offered to pay him a nominal fee, plus a city lot. He refused. Embittered, he spent his last years in poverty and was buried on the private estate of a friend, just outside the District's northeastern boundary.

Despite problems with L'Enfant and the predicted land speculations, Ellicott completed a map in 1792. Generally following L'Enfant's specifications, the overall design featured square and rectangular blocks. The city was divided into four quadrants along the plans of commissioners Carroll, Johnson, and Stuart. North and south streets were numbered, and east and west streets were lettered. As the city expanded northward, letter names

Federal Hall in New York City was an early home of Congress (1785–1790) and the site of Washington's 1789 inaugural.

were followed by alphabetically arranged two-syllable names such as Quincy or Randolph. Three-syllable names, such as Tewkesbury and Underwood, were then used, followed by an alphabetical list of tree names and names of other flora, extending to the District Line. Crossing the entire pattern were diagonal avenues named after states. The quadrant initials NW, NE, SE, and SW are part of all Washington addresses today.

The main part of the city began in the northwest area. Wherever avenues intersected, small parks with statues and fountains, creating "circles," were designed to increase the city's beauty, immortalize national heroes, and honor states of the Union. With the advent of modern transportation, they also complicated traffic.

The larger circles present motorists with concentric traffic lanes that have several access points to streets that feed into the circles. Several turns around the circle are often required for the novice Washington driver to find a way out, particularly when the feeder streets alternate one-way traffic. It is entirely possible to become quite lost in Washington's circles.

Initially, two central features of L'Enfant's plan, the president's palace and the Capitol, received the most attention. A contest was held offering $500 and a city lot for the best design for each. An English physician and amateur architect, William Thornton, won the prize for the Capitol, though his entry was received late. The design of James Hoban was chosen for the palace.

Although expanded in stages by different architects, Thornton's basic concepts for the Capitol endured. His design called for a square central structure linking rectangular north and south wings. The main ornamentation for his simple but stately Capitol was to be columns fronting the entry and a low dome atop the midsection. Thronton had great hopes for his concept. But, like L'Enfant, his tenure was cut short by arguments on how the plans would be executed.

As they reached completion, actual construction progress was slow. Work began on Pennsylvania Avenue with the cutting of trees and brush. In the first capital parade, in 1793, George Washington led District of Columbia, Virginia, and Maryland masons to lay a Capitol cornerstone. The avenue, coined the "Great Serbonian Bog," seemed virtually unchanged.

Marchers trudged through the murk, crossing Tiber Creek leading to the Capitol over a log bridge.

Landowners continued to plant crops in the area until Pennsylvania Avenue had been completely cleared. President Washington, eager for the city's advancement, rushed his commissioners along in the project.

Building Lags

All the capital's roadways were in bad condition. Tiber Creek, which has since become Constitution Avenue, would often flood, making adjacent streets unusable. One commentator noted that from the foot of Capitol Hill westward, the area was almost impassable for vehicles of any kind. Mud, bushes, thorns, briars, and other obstacles made walking difficult in some places. On the south side, clumps of thornbushes were so thick that they were likely cut down with scythes to enable the workers to make a footway to Fifteenth Street. The only buildings there, however, were a coach stop and a three-story building sheltering a tinner's shop.

Still behind schedule in 1798, sites for other government office buildings needed to be settled. The new President, John Adams, objected to Washington's intention of placing the buildings close to the President's House. Instead, he preferred a site closer to the Capitol and the workings of government. Deferring to Washington's plan, commissioners overruled Adams and broke ground for what would be a three-story brick executive office building adjacent to the presidential mansion. This structure was placed where today's Treasury Building now stands. Another building, an exact copy, was to be constructed on the opposite side of the Executive Mansion.

Executive branch staff began to arrive from Philadelphia in June 1800. President Adams also made a brief trip to Washington, D.C., at that time to inspect the White House and the original Treasury Building.

Even with continued setbacks, members of Congress and a small group of government employees arrived from Philadelphia in November 1800. Instead of great plans fulfilled, the newcomers found barely a skeleton of a city. The President's wife, Abigail Adams, passed through such wilderness en route that her coach got lost and she had to hire a guide

The President's House was burned by the British in 1814 during the War of 1812.

to find the way. Upon arrival, Abigail faced an almost barren swamp where about 3,000 Americans had already come to seek fortunes that hardly seemed attainable.

The exterior of the President's House was complete, but the interior lacked common conveniences. Outside the house, litter was strewn everywhere, the product of the ongoing construction within. Bankrupt land speculators had left abandoned houses nearby, further marring the view. Hardly any shops or occupied houses could be seen. Without lights, roads, or walkways, venturing out was difficult. Complete wilderness lay beyond the proposed Mall. It was a far cry from bustling Philadelphia.

On Nov. 22, 1800, John Adams delivered his first Washington message to Congress in an unfinished Capitol. Despite its problems, he knew Washington, D.C., was the future lifeline of the nation. He spoke of great hopes for it as the "residence of virtue and happiness." But as Congress trudged through the mud to a reception at the President's House, promises of future comforts seemed remote.

Only the north wing of the Capitol was complete, so the 106 members of the House of Representatives, 32 senators, Library of Congress personnel, justices of the Supreme Court

of the United States, and the justices of the Circuit Court were cramped into a single crowded space. The Supreme Court justices found the Capitol basement so stifling, they often heard cases in a nearby tavern.

Members of Congress found living accommodations equally disagreeable. There were few boarding houses and even fewer taverns. Ten to 20 legislators boarded together in one house. The sorry living conditions prompted Oliver Wolcott, Jr., secretary of the treasury, to compare the existence of the members of Congress to that of monks in a monastery.

Rain—and there is plenty of it in the District—made the bad roads worse. When the sun came out, mosquitoes flocked to the area, breeding malaria. As the mud dried in the heat, dust filled the air. Then the cycle was renewed.

"Potomac fever," a term that was to become associated with an assortment of maladies in the capital, raged. Conditions were so bad that most government workers and officials left their families at home. Congressional sessions were kept short so those involved in the government could remain in "civilized " surroundings as long as possible.

The nearest comfortable lodgings were in Georgetown, on the southern edge of Washington along the Potomac. But in those days the thriving colonial shipping port was a long, rough ride from the Capitol, crossing Rock Creek. Still, many lawmakers saw this quaint metropolis as a haven from the coarse accommodations of Washington, D.C.

Comfort in Georgetown

While the District would become known as a "city of streets and no houses," Georgetown was a "city of houses and no streets." Narrow thoroughfares were of cobblestone. Brick sidewalks were lined with shuttered, ivy-covered houses that boasted carefully manicured, enclosed gardens. Here suffering officials found respite.

Georgetown, annexed by the District of Columbia in 1871, became recognized for its historical and architectural importance even in these early years. George Washington reached the agreement with landowners for the site of the permanent capital in a Georgetown inn. Also in Georgetown, William Thornton, the first Capitol architect, designed the famous Tudor Place for the son of the port's first major, Thomas Peter. In 1805, Peter moved into the house with his bride, Martha

Parke Custis, the granddaughter of Martha Washington.

More diversified business followed the establishment of the government in Washington. Most of the commercial growth occurred away from the Capitol, up Pennsylvania Avenue. At the start, there were only a few shops and some lumberyards. Members of Congress boarded at inns or taverns on the avenue. Away from domestic responsibilities, they were free to discuss Congressional issues there. The Indian Queen Hotel was a focal point for much government activity.

The National Intelligencer moved from Philadelphia to Washington to report government news. To acquire more accurate stories, the newspaper was allowed to station one of its reporters on the floor of the Senate and one in the House of Representatives.

Jefferson's presidency from 1801 to 1809 saw many changes in Washington, D.C. New structures included the House of Representatives wing of the Capitol, churches, military barracks, and lovely houses such as Octagon House, where James and Dolley Madison lived for a time after the British burned the Executive Mansion in the War of 1812.

Although the city was growing, Jefferson realized that conditions had to improve in

By 1848, gas lamps illuminated Pennsylvania Avenue in front of the White House.

The Indian Queen Hotel was the focal point of much government activity in the early 1800's.

order to quell proposals to find a new site for the capital. Foreign diplomats rated Washington as a hardship post, even a dangerous place in which to socialize. Upon returning from the President's House, officials would often lose their way. Reports had it that lost visitors could spend until daybreak in their carriages, weaving through bogs and gullies in search of Capitol Hill, only 1 mile (1.6 kilometers) away.

Congress approved funds in 1803 for improvements in the capital. One-fourth of the money was set aside for Pennsylvania Avenue alone. The government's allocation was the first of many to benefit Washington, D.C., in the following years.

James Hoban, architect for the presidential mansion, ordered that lighting be installed for the "upper avenue" near his project. Jefferson directed that Lombardy poplar trees be planted at curbs and down the avenue median. Earlier he had tried to save groves of tulip trees, which were the only natural beauty in the city, but they were chopped for firewood, as were some of his poplars.

Despite the capital's troubled state, presidential protocol was being established. Visitors had bowed to Presidents Washington and Adams. Jefferson preferred to shake hands, and so set a precedent for all his successors.

Jefferson was inaugurated twice with lit-

tle fanfare. But President James Madison led the first Inaugural Parade in 1809. He had a military escort that moved up Pennsylvania Avenue to the White House. Although invited to ride along, Jefferson declined, wishing for Madison to receive all the honors of the day. After the inauguration, the first inaugural ball took place at Long's Hotel, where the Library of Congress now stands.

In 1812, Christ Church, Capitol Hill, founded the Congressional Cemetery 1½ miles (2.4 kilometers) from the Capitol, for the graves of members of Congress who died in office. It is also the burial place for William Thornton and John Philip Sousa, American bandmaster and composer who led the U.S. Marine Band in the late 1800's.

Guarding the gravestones is a monument to Robert Mills, the architect who designed the Washington Monument, Treasury Building, and Old Post Office. Since 1973, the cemetery, declared a national landmark, has been maintained by the U.S. National Park Service.

Tradition mingled with pride as Washington developed. However, progress was dampened as the United States was drawn into a conflict between France and Great Britain during Madison's administration. The United States tried to stay neutral. But both sides were ruining U.S. shipping profits with trade blockades. The British navy was also stopping American ships and forcing U. S. sailors into British service.

Finally, Congress voted by a narrow margin to declare war in Great Britain. The British foreign minister had agreed two days earlier to stop interfering with U. S. trade, but President Madison did not receive the notice in time to call off U.S. involvement in what became the War of 1812.

The Capital Burns

Much of the fighting occurred at sea, although British Redcoats appeared from New Orleans to Canada. To punish American successes in Canada, British troops set out to seize the U.S. capital. General Robert Ross led land forces, while Rear Admiral George Cockburn directed the British marines. They combined forces in Maryland, proceeding to Bladensburg on foot. The better-trained Redcoats easily broke through American lines and continued to Washington. They bypassed Fort Washington, built on the Maryland side of the Potomac to protect the capital.

The Madisons and the Cabinet fled to Virginia. Dolley Madison heroically saved the famous Gilbert Stuart portrait of George Washington, refusing to leave the White House without it, even with British troops almost in the city. Securely fastened to a wall, the painting was finally ripped out by her order. She then took it with her as she fled in her carriage. The portrait hangs today in the White House.

The British set fire to the Capitol, the President's House, and other public buildings, as well as the office of *The National Intelligencer* newspaper. Only a severe rainstorm save the city from total destruction. The British then moved on to Baltimore, where they were defeated on land and water. After their loss, they were ready to negotiate peace. President Madison signed the Treaty of Ghent in Octagon House.

Washington lay in ruins. Damage to government property was great. Only the Post Office and Patent Office survived when William Thornton convinced a British major to save the building where they were located.

Equally hurt was the nation's pride. Members of Congress again considered moving the capital to a spot that offered more protection. Instead, they voted large sums of money for rebuilding.

In the fall of 1814 Congress met in the Patent Office Building. From 1815 to 1819, they met in the hastily constructed "Brick Capitol." Private citizens had funded the construction of the building, which was erected within six months. The Capitol reopened in 1819.

President and Dolley Madison moved to Octagon House on 18th Street and New York Avenue, then later to a house on 19th Street, while the President's House was being repaired. Octagon House was built by Thornton for Colonel John Tayloe, a wealthy planter and horse breeder. Coaxed by George Washington to build in Washington instead of Philadelphia, Tayloe wanted a home where he and his daughter could entertain distinguished friends. Octagon House became one of the most fashionable homes in the District of Columbia. Made of brick, it had six sides, rather than eight, as its name implies. As the capital's first famous hostess, Dolley Madison entertained many notable visitors there.

Through the years, Octagon House's historical importance grew. It was a Civil War military hospital and a school. Most recently, it has served as part of headquarters for the American Institute of Architects and has been restored as a museum.

In the years following the War of 1812, Washington was in conflict. Immigrants from war-wracked Europe flooded to the United States, settling mainly in Northern cities. Their numbers changed the character of the work force there. Southern states continued to rely on slave labor. Washington, D.C., has been a major port for slave ships, and slave auctions were held where Potomac Park now stands.

By February 1819, debates rang on Capitol Hill with regard to whether Missouri should be admitted to the Union as a slave state. Threats of dissolving the Union were countered with firm stands on freedom for all. The Missouri Compromise of 1820 was received as a temporary settlement for the nation. Missouri was admitted as a slave state and Maine as a free state. The Compromise also banned slavery from the Louisiana Purchase north of Missouri's southern border— 36° 30' north latitude—except in Missouri.

For the capital, the question was never really settled. By 1830, the number of free blacks in the District of Columbia equaled that of slaves. Fearful whites passed laws prohibiting blacks to congregate. After Nat

Construction of the iron Capitol dome can be seen in the background as Lincoln is inaugurated on March 4, 1861.

Turner's uprising, in which about 60 whites were killed in Virginia in 1831, a 10 P.M. curfew was enforced, and black preachers were forbidden to hold religious meetings.

Rebuilding the Capital

As the slavery questing dragged on, so did the job of rebuilding Washington. Congress seemed reluctant to spend money for much-needed renovation in the city.

The President's buff-colored mansion received its first coast of white paint as its renovation neared completion. It was ready for the Monroes to move in by 1817. The Capitol took longer. It had consisted of wings for the Senate and House of Representatives that were linked by a covered wooden walkway. The entire structure demanded total reconditioning. Through the years, contributions by some of the world's finest painters, sculptors, and architects would make it a shrine to the art and history of a young nation.

After the War of 1812, Benjamin Henry Latrobe, a Britisher, sought to rebuild the Capitol according to Thornton's original plan. President Jefferson had appointed Latrobe surveyor of public buildings in 1803. His priority became the Capitol. Latrobe's talent was to be revealed in intricate cornstalk and tobacco leaf patterns adorning inside columns of the Capitol. These motifs represented the fruits of American toil.

Latrobe's duties went to Charles Bulfinch in 1817. He was the first native American architect involved in Washington construction. Under Bulfinch's supervision, the Senate and House chambers were restored in time for the 1819 Congressional session. He then replaced the wooden walkway with a central Rotunda sheltered by a low, copper-covered wooden dome.

Through his efforts, four bas-reliefs—carvings or sculpture—decorated the walls over the four doors leading to the Rotunda. All four sculptures have Indian themes. Over the east door is *The Landing of the Pilgrims*, and the south door has *Conflict Between Daniel Boone and the Indians*. To the west is *Rescue of Captain John Smith*, while to the north stands *Penn's Treaty with the Indians*.

Less Land for the Capital

By the 1840's, Washington, D.C., had only about 50,000 persons. Only a small part of the area was built up. As a result, in 1846 Congress returned to Virginia the land the state had given to the federal government for the capital.

Congress itself grew faster. By 1850, its new chambers were too small. Funds were allocated for architect Thomas U. Walter to extend the building. He created the magnificent Capitol we see today. Future artists increased its beauty and added to the symbolism of the Capitol.

The original dome appeared skimpy in contrast to the enlarged wings. So Walter replaced the former wooden dome with a larger, cast-iron one more than 130 feet (40 meters) in diameter, weighing almost 9 million pounds (4 million kilograms), and rising more than 180 feet (55 meters) above the Rotunda floor. Thirty-six columns around the lower portion were added. Smaller columns enveloped a lantern.

To stand proud atop the Capitol dome went the Statue of Freedom, 19.5 feet (5.9 meters) high. An outstanding American sculptor, Thomas Crawford, carved the 15,000-pound (6,804-kilogram) bronze statue to symbolize Armed Liberty protecting America, with "heavenly" stars encircling the statue's feathered helmet. The draped figure leans on a sword with the right hand and holds a wreath and shield in the left.

Under the dome, the circular Rotunda, about 95 feet (29 meters) in diameter, leads to the House and Senate wings of the Capitol. Decorating much of the Capitol's dome, rooms, and hallways are frescoes painted by Italian-born Constantino Brumidi. Brumidi labored for 25 years for an average of $3,200 per year while Presidents Franklin Pierce, James Buchanan, Abraham Lincoln, Andrew Johnson, Ulysses S. Grant, and Rutherford B. Hayes directed government business. His brightly colored floral designs and historic murals blend mythology, industry, and nature to illuminate the glory of the nation.

Four of the eight large paintings in the Rotunda were done by John Trumbull, who fought alongside George Washington in the Revolutionary War. They are of special historical significance because they portray the nation's early settlement and fight for independence. Another painting, *The Baptism of Pocahontas*, also attracts attention. People want to see the "Indian with six toes."

Many statues line the Rotunda wall. The most famous is a marble statue of the "Great Emancipator," Abraham Lincoln. Vinnie Ream, at 17, had been granted permission by President Lincoln to sketch him during his daily half-hour rest period. When he was assassinated, the unknown artist created the solemn massive statue of the national hero.

Beneath the Rotunda lie several monuments few visitors see, including a grand tomb intended for George Washington that Congress ordered. But the Washington family opposed moving his body from his Mount Vernon home.

Horatio Greenough's classical marble statue of George Washington adorned like a Greek god was also part of the planned memorial. It was installed in the Rotunda and later moved outdoors. Today the statue is part of the Smithsonian Institution's collection.

Lush gardens contrast with the simple elegance of the White House.

Statuary Hall, which was the original House of Representatives, abounds in presidential history. James Madison took his oath of office there. A bronze disc, or plate, marks the spot where John Quincy Adams, serving as a member of Congress after retirement from the presidency, collapsed before his death. In 1864, a bill was passed designating the hall as the National Hall of Statuary and inviting donations of bronze or marble statues of distinguished Americans.

In the walnut-paneled House of Representatives, the President gives his State of the Union address to both houses behind a gray marble speaker's platform flanked by portraits of the Marquis de Lafayette and George Washington. Above the spectators' gallery, under a border of state seals, are profiles of famous lawmakers ranging from Hammurabi to Jefferson. Behind the House is the Speaker's Lobby and a House Reading Room.

The marble-columned Old Senate Chamber was used by the Senate until 1859 and the Supreme Court until 1935. Beyond the Old Chamber lies the newer Senate Chamber, where each political party has its own side of the room and senators are seated by seniority from front to back. Just off the chamber, lobbyists congregate in the carpeted Senate Reception Room to rally support for their proposals.

The Changing City

L'Enfant's grand plan included an uninterrupted view down Pennsylvania Avenue between the Capitol and White House. But that dream was shattered by the building of a new U.S. Treasury to replace the one destroyed by a fire in 1833.

The site of the new Treasury Building was ordered by Andrew Jackson. Since 1842, the classic Greek structure has jutted across Pennsylvania Avenue. Beyond the Treasury Building's stately columned entry are the offices of the secretary of the treasury, whose various duties include overseeing the minting, payment, and collection of U.S. money. There are funds protected in secure vaults under the building. Completion of the Treasury Building symbolized the idea of business as government that became firmly imbedded during President Jackson's administration.

A railroad terminal was built at the foot of Capitol Hill at this time. Some residents opposed it as unsightly, but others remarked on its potential profitability rather than questioning its beauty.

Washington's appearance improved little, but Congress accepted greater responsibility for Pennsylvania Avenue. In 1832, the House approved surfacing and guttering the avenue, plus removing the decimated remnants of dead poplars. Outer rows of poplars were replaced by elms for shade.

The capital's social structure changed with Andrew Jackson, whose name would become closely linked with the "spoils system," whereby new appointments are made for federal jobs with each administration. Jackson replaced more jobholders than ever before, and he made no excuses for his patronage. Instead, he boldly defended the merits of the system.

From then on, officeholders thought of themselves more as passing through Washington, rather than as being a permanent part of its organization. The old-line socially elite, however, gravitated to an area called President's Square just north of the White House. After the Marquis de Lafayette's visit to Washington in 1824, the area was named Lafayette Square in his honor.

In 1816, only St. John's Church, designed by Latrobe, sat with the White House on the square. Number 54 stamps the pew offered to President Madison by a church committee. The number has been reserved for each President after that time. Since its completion, nearly every President has attended some service at St. John's. Franklin Delano Roosevelt prayed there before three of his four inaugurations.

The highlight of Lafayette Square is a controversial tribute to Andrew Jackson. Clark Mills sculpted this equestrian statue from a cannon captured by "Old Hickory" in the War of 1812. To sketch the horse, Mills supposedly bought a Virginia thoroughbred and trained him to rear. The resulting statue won acclaim as an artistic and engineering feat. Unimpressed observers thought of it as an impossible person on a more impossible horse with a most impossible tail.

Many luxurious homes have come to Lafayette Square and gone, and stories persist of the people from "official Washington." It was here that Dolley Madison lived after her husband's death in 1837. She was a frequent White House guest and called there regularly on New Year's Day until her death in 1849.

An imposing statue of Abraham Lincoln sits in the center of the Lincoln Memorial.

Commodore Stephen Decatur built the first private residence on the square with money won for his bravery fighting pirates on the Barbary Coast. He bought a number of lots and ordered Latrobe to design a home on the northwest corner of one plot. For a year, he and Mrs. Decatur held elegant affairs for affluent politicians, including a ball for one of President Monroe's daughters. Then, in 1820, Decatur was killed in a duel.

Honor among the well-to-do cost many their lives on the square. In 1859, member of Congress Daniel Sickles crossed Lafayette Square to shoot Philip Barton Key, son of the author of the "Star-Spangled Banner." The

incident did not hamper Sickle's career. He distinguished himself as a general and diplomat, living to old age.

As Washington matured politically and socially, efforts to improve the capital culturally were realized as well. For an institution to cultivate knowledge, an eccentric English scientist, James Smithson, left his entire fortune to the United States: 105 bags of gold coins. His gift was deposited in the U.S. Treasury. The gold arrived in 1838, along with Smithson's library and collection of minerals.

Congress debated what to do with the money for eight years. Members considered

returning the gift. Finally, Congress used it to begin what became known as the Smithsonian Institution.

The original Smithsonian building, located on the Mall, was designed by James Renwick, Jr., to look like a Norman castle. The red sandstone structure has nine ornate towers and holds Smithson's tomb. For 30 years the "Castle on the Mall," also called the "Nation's Attic," was the sole repository for the country, the site of all institution activities and displays. The building currently houses the administration offices of the institution and serves as the institution's main visitor center.

Today the Smithsonian manages numerous museums and galleries, plus the National Zoological Park. Its collection of items goes into the tens of millions.

"City of Magnificent Intentions"

In 1847, when Congressional freshman Abraham Lincoln stayed at Mrs. Sprigg's Boardinghouse, where the Library of Congress now stands, Washington streets were cluttered with chickens, pigs, and geese. There were slave pens 1 mile (1.6 kilometers) from the Hill. Underground Railroad stations helped slaves escape to free territory. The city's canal emitted a foul odor. Charles Dickens, upon visiting Washington, called it the "City of Magnificent Intentions."

Attempts to improve the Mall were short-lived. President Millard Fillmore commissioned landscape architect Andrew Jackson Downing to beautify the Mall and White House grounds in the early 1850's. Resulting plans featuring winding paths and a triumphal marble arch over Pennsylvania Avenue near the White House greatly deviated from L'Enfant's layout. Downing died in 1852. The Civil War, plus political and financial roadblocks, stymied his plans.

The Missouri Compromise did not hold back the tides of war. Even before the 1860 election, many Southern leaders threatened to have their states secede, or withdraw, from the Union. After Abraham Lincoln won, South Carolina seceded in December, followed by other Southern states. President James Buchan-

The National Gallery of Art's East Building houses paintings and sculpture.

an allowed them to withdraw without resistance. Six weeks after President Lincoln took office, the Union North and Confederate South were at war.

Washington, D.C., became a military camp for the next four years. Defense forts, like restored Fort Stevens on the Northwest side, formed a band surrounding the city. Landscaped parks and squares became tent cities housing training troops. Regiments drilled on Pennsylvania Avenue. Ground that held the beginnings of the Washington Monument housed slaughtering pens for the cattle needed to feed hungry troops. Other open land was used for stabling thousands of horses, some of which pulled carts carrying dead, sick, and wounded to hospitals.

Brothels flourished with the overload of military and civilians. Blacks fleeing slavery also flooded the District of Columbia. Space was at a premium. Even jails were full. The population climbed from about 75,000 in 1860 to about 131,700 by 1870. And slums abounded. The worst, known as "Murder Bay," covered the area where the Department of Commerce now stands.

The Capitol renovation was nearing completion. Now it was turned into quarters for the first Northern troops reaching Washington. Soldiers slept everywhere, including under House and Senate desks, while officers occupied committee rooms. *Harper's Weekly* reported that the galleries under the Senate chamber were filled with barrels of flour, beef, poultry, and hams. Basement committee rooms were converted into a bakery with room-sized ovens. Sights and sounds of the capital in war so stirred Julia Ward Howe, a writer and social reformer, that she composed the words for the "Battle Hymn of the Republic" while staying in a room at the Willard Hotel.

Robert E. Lee's Arlington estate overlooked the Washington encampments. In the years that followed, Arlington National Cemetery, set on land which had been part of this estate, became a national shrine for all the nation's war dead. A white sea of equally spaced stone markers fills a large area of the original estate. The Tomb of the Unknown Soldier holds the body of an unidentified fighter from World War I. In front of this tomb are two flat marble slabs marking the tombs for two more unknown soldiers—those who perished in World War II and the Korean War.

The Civil War dragged on until April 9,

Marble columns and elaborate decoration adorn the Great Hall of the Thomas Jefferson Building, one of three buildings that make up the Library of Congress. In addition to providing research and reference assistance to the U.S. Congress, the library also serves other government agencies and the general public.

1865, when General Lee surrendered to General Grant at Appomattox Court House, Va. Jubilant crowds lighted bonfires in the streets of Washington. Five days later, as a weary President Lincoln watched a play at Ford's Theatre, actor John Wilkes Booth assassinated him. Thousands of tearful mourners followed Lincoln's black hearse pulled by six gray horses. The procession went down Pennsylvania Avenue from the White House to the Capitol, where six weeks earlier, Lincoln had been inaugurated for his second term.

Ford's Theatre has been restored to its original appearance, along with the home of tailor William Petersen, where the wounded President was carried on that night. The murder pistol and other Lincoln memorabilia are displayed at a museum in the theater. The site of Mary Surratt's boarding house is in northwest Washington. Here, Booth plotted Lincoln's murder. For her part in the conspiracy, Surratt was executed.

Post-Civil War years were laden with graft and corruption in the capital. Stories spread of the scandalous state of the capital. Criminals and the unemployed gathered in old cavalry stables. Streets were trampled by military divisions. The city was badly in need of repair.

Although various public buildings were under construction, funds for local expenses had always been scarce in the capital. But in 1871, Congress moved to improve the city's condition. The area of the District, including Georgetown, was to be combined under a territorial form of government. Then, President Grant appointed a governor, an 11-person upper house, and a Board of Public Works to beautify Washington. District elections chose members of a lower-level House of Delegates and one nonvoting delegate to Congress.

A New Washington

Sewer, road, and sidewalk construction relieved problems that had plagued Washington since its birth. Run-down, vacant buildings were razed, disease-ridden marshes were filled, and street lights were installed. More trees were planted on Pennsylvania Avenue and along other streets. The city was alive with the sounds of work crews that provided jobs for many unemployed persons.

Opposition existed, however, to the plans of Alexander Robey Shepherd, Vice-President of the Board of Public Works and the force behind the renewal program. Complaints led to repeated investigations for excessive spending. President Grant appointed Shepherd governor of the District of Columbia in 1873, but, eventually, he was forced out of office. Although cleared of any wrongdoing, Shepherd spent fifteen years in self-imposed exile in Mexico.

After his departure, the District of Columbia government was reorganized under tighter Congressional control. Shepherd finally returned to Washington to a hero's welcome in 1887. Realizing his accomplishments, appreciative citizens gave him a parade up Pennsylvania Avenue. In front of the District Building today stands a statue of Shepherd.

After its face-lift, more of Washington's government officials wanted to settle there. Real estate became big business, and the population reached 200,000 by 1880. On major avenues, embassy delegations, business tycoons, and members of Congress occupied elegant mansions. Tree-lined Massachusetts Avenue had so many embassies it earned its nickname, "Embassy Row." Travelers admired the sparkling white buildings, lush parks, and shady, paved streets.

One of the spectacular projects to be completed during this era was the noble Washington Monument, located west of the Capitol. The Washington National Monument Society, created in 1833, was able to get the project through by soliciting funds and prodding Congress. The monument was completed on Dec. 6, 1884. Its marble shaft towers about 555.5 feet (169 meters) high and shines like a beacon for the entire District of Columbia.

Robert Mills won the contest for the monument's design originally, but it was altered through the many years of construction, which began in 1848. Nearly 200 marble blocks were donated by individuals, municipalities, states, societies, and other countries to build the memorial.

Work on the monument was halted due to lack of funds, construction disputes, and the Civil War. By the time it resumed, the marble used in the initial construction was unavailable, so slabs of a slightly different color had to be used. The color break is distinct partway up the shaft.

Built in the aftermath of Shepherd's grand plans, the new Library of Congress was expanded to keep Congress well informed and to keep up with the growing collection. The library is housed in three buildings just east of the Capitol. Past and present members of Congress receive books and other materials by a cable conveyor running through an underground tunnel from the library's basement to the Capi-

tol's receiving room. Others pursuing serious research have access to the library's more than 160 million items, which include books, magazines, films, microfiche, recordings, and Braille materials for the blind.

The Library of Congress houses one of the greatest collections in the world, and it grows by 12,000 items per working day. The library owns the largest collection of incunabula (books printed before 1501) in the Western Hemisphere, with more than 5,700 books. And its collection of Chinese, Japanese, Korean, Polish, and Russian materials is the largest outside those countries.

The library was completed in 1897. In the main reading room, a bright, gold-leaf rosette dome encloses curved card catalogs and mahogany reading desks. Marble columns encircle the room, and stained-glass windows add to the quiet work atmosphere.

The library's corridors house exhibits of rare books, maps, prints, and manuscripts, as well as treasures such as a Stradivarius violin and the famous Gutenberg Bible, one of the first books printed from movable type.

Since 1870, the Library of Congress has protected the works of authors, musicians, artists, and filmmakers against illegal copying by registering claims for copyright. The library adds to its collection of books and other works by choosing from among the items sent to it in accordance with copyright registration requirements.

The United States Senate Page School is located in the library's main building. Young people between 14 and 18 years old attend classes there from 6:10 to 9:45 a.m. each day before going to work running errands for House or Senate members.

Part of the library's responsibility until 1935 was the National Archives. The federal government has required preservation of its records since the first Continental Congress met in 1774. Historical documents, including census lists going back to 1790, are now stored in an ornate, columned structure. Enshrined within its solemn rotunda is a bronze altar encasing the Declaration of Independence, the Bill of Rights, and the Constitution of the United States. Precious, aging papers such as these are protected in thermoglass cases filled with helium. Each night, they are lowered into a steel and concrete vault below the floor.

History is told in the documents and personal papers of famous people displayed around the room. Federal documents and drawings are stored in steel cabinets or in stacked areas with shelving systems where objects are placed in acid-neutral cardboard boxes.

More Dissatisfaction with Capital

With all its changes, the capital still was unsatisfactory to many. Congress had spent money mainly for structures in which it could conduct business: buildings for the library, the post office, the treasury, and the departments of state, war, and navy.

Prominent residents were appalled at the terrible condition of the Mall by the 1900's. Senator James McMillan from Michigan was one of the most vocal critics. As chair of the Senate District Committee, he convinced Congress in 1901 to appoint two architects, a landscape architect, and a sculptor to evaluate the city's park system and guide its renovation. Charles McKim from New York, one of the preeminent architects of the time; Daniel Burnham, architect and director of the World's Columbian Exposition; Frederick Law Olmsted, Jr., landscapist; and Augustus Saint-Gaudens, a noted American sculptor, comprised the renowned Senate Park Commission, a four-member body that became known as the McMillan Commission. They worked for a year without pay.

McMillan funded the commission's trips to study parks and buildings in Europe's finest cities at his own expense. After considerable research, the team submitted a report supporting L'Enfant's basic concepts. They confirmed that the original plan of the city of Washington was sound, and considered departures from that plan as regrettable. The commission recommended remedies for the departures wherever possible.

Because the commission thought so highly of L'Enfant's plan, city leaders wanted to honor the architect who had died disgraced. They raised L'Enfant's body in 1909. The architect was then reburied in a grave in Arlington Cemetery, overlooking the city he created.

Some members of Congress balked at the cost of the commission's proposed project. However, many of the committee's recommendations were soon implemented. The approved project took decades to complete.

Train tracks were removed from the Mall, restoring an unobstructed view of the Capitol. Swampland was filled and landscaped to the Potomac's shores. Union Station, completed in 1907, replaced the Mall depot and others in the city. Daniel Burnham designed the station complex to have an immense plaza with landscaping and statues surrounded by Greek columns facing the Capitol. A scaled-down version of the complex cost nearly $22 million. It had a central arched pavilion guarded in front by an overpowering statue of Columbus, set in a fountain. Statues illustrating fire, electricity, freedom, inspiration (knowledge), agriculture, and mechanics stood at the passenger entrance.

When railroad owners threatened to demolish the building in the 1960's, the gov-

---

Do You Know?

1. Where was the first national capital under the Constitution?
2. How did Dolley Madison win praise during the War of 1812?
3. What is Octagon House?
4. What is sometimes called Uncle Sam's Company Town?
5. What President got lost trying to find the White House?
6. What branch of the federal government met over a market, in the Capitol basement, and in a tavern in the early days of the Republic?
7. What election was the first in which Washingtonians were able to vote for President?
8. What is the name of the statue on top of the Capitol dome?
9. Why was the Virginia portion of the national capital returned to that state in the mid-1800's?
10. Why does the Washington Monument show a distinct break in color in the stone used to build it?

Answers: (1) New York City; (2) by saving Gilbert Stuart's portrait of George Washington from the White House before the British burned it in the War of 1812; (3) a six-sided house where the Madisons lived for a time after the White House was burned; (4) Washington, D.C.; (5) J. Adams, because the area was a wilderness; (6) the Supreme Court; (7) the 1964 election; (8) the Statue of Freedom; (9) because of the District's relatively slow growth; (10) Construction was renewed on the monument in 1880 after a 25-year break due in part to the Civil War; the marble used in earlier construction could not be matched.

ernment gave it landmark status and turned it into the National Visitor Center. The Visitor Center was a failure; the building began to decay and was subsequently closed for safety reasons. The building, which lies just north of the Capitol, has since been reopened as a combination shopping center, entertainment center, office center, and train station. The station serves passenger trains that run between Washington and other parts of the country.

By 1908, seven new buildings had been completed in the capital—the District Building, the Department of Agriculture, the Army War College, office buildings for the House and Senate, an additional National Museum, and the District Public Library.

Meanwhile, the Washington leadership was changing with the Administrations of Theodore Roosevelt, William Howard Taft, and Woodrow Wilson. There was a growing inter-

est in the arts and great concern for public welfare. Congress appointed the Fine Arts Commission and later the National Capital Park and Planning Commission to carry out the aims of the McMillan Commission.

World War I dulled the enthusiasm for city improvements. As a center for Allied activities, Washington saw troops march down Pennsylvania Avenue once again. This time Washingtonians sang "Tipperary" or songs about the Kaiser. People from all over the country came to assist in the war effort. Makeshift office and living quarters were thrown together. Some would remain for decades.

After the Armistice, President Wilson's debilitating stroke slowed the wheels of government. One excitement for the city was the long-awaited construction of the Lincoln Memorial. A commanding 19-foot (5.8-meter) statue for the memorial offered an excellent

Just across from the White House is Lafayette Square, named after the Revolutionary War hero Marquis de Lafayette.

likeness of the "Great Emancipator" seated on a marble armchair.

Sculptor Daniel Chester French carved Lincoln's statue after he had completed a commission at nearby Gallaudet College for the deaf. To understand his work there, he had learned sign language. French was so fascinated by it that he is said to have carved the shape of Lincoln's left hand to be a manual *A*. The right hand has a slightly extended thumb and forefinger, suggesting the manual *L*. Thus, French may have shown Lincoln signing his own initials. Other interpretations of the hands' positions include French's possible intention to show the President in both a relaxed and tense mood.

Sheltering the Lincoln statue is an open Greek marble temple. Thirty-six columns representing the states in the Union at the time of Lincoln's death support its frame. On the inside walls, Lincoln's second inaugural address and the Gettysburg Address are etched in bronze. Lincoln looks out to the peaceful Reflecting Pool, which extends toward the Washington Monument. His troubled expression mirrors the troubled times both when he lived and when he was honored.

Continuing Growth

Washington, D.C., did not come alive again until Wilson left office and President and Mrs. Warren G. Harding opened the White House for guests. Theirs was an era of gaiety and prosperity. The Hardings entertained at huge garden parties. This was during the 1920's, when the District of Columbia's population soared to nearly 500,000 and the booming construction industry reached a peak. Congress approved a multimillion dollar proposal for a public buildings program to carry out the McMillan and L'Enfant plans.

President Herbert Hoover was especially supportive of the program. When the stock market crashed in 1929 and the Great Depression began, work still continued. Under Hoover and, later, under Franklin Roosevelt, many of the projects were completed in the 1930's.

Plush apartments and hotels were built to accommodate the influx of government workers attracted by the expanded Roosevelt Administration. Parks became a place for picnics, sports, and concerts. Rock Creek Park was improved and expanded through northwest

Washington. Arlington Memorial Bridge, leading to the cemetery, was erected over the Potomac. Four equestrian statues decorate the bridge. Designed and modeled by Americans, they were cast in bronze and gilded in Italy as a gift to the United States from the Italian people.

Across the Tidal Basin in southwest Washington, the Jefferson Memorial was set in a serene grove of cherry trees. A controversy developed when plans included removing some of the trees in order to make room for the memorial. Misgivings among protestors were quieted when the announcement came that many more cherry trees would be planted to replace those removed.

The Jefferson Memorial was begun in 1938 and completed in 1942. Its outer dome and columns reflect the design of Jefferson's Monticello home, which he designed. Inside the memorial, a statue of Jefferson in knee breeches and a fur coat stands on a pedestal. The coat represents a gift from a noted Polish engineer and patriot, Thaddeus Kosciusko. Jefferson valued the coat and wore it frequently.

Jefferson's words, which he helped to make the philosophy of the nation, are inscribed around the base of the dome: "I have sworn upon the altar of God eternal hostility against every form of tyranny over the mind of man."

Another proposal acted upon a this time involved banding office buildings for many agencies into a single right triangle, which became known as the Federal Triangle. The wedge, formed by Constitution and Pennsylvania avenues, would replace the old commercial center. All buildings were to be six stories high and similar in design. In order to construct the complex, existing buildings were to be torn down.

Thousands work in the Federal Triangle buildings, which are gigantic monuments to big government. They include the Federal Trade Commission, the National Archives, the Department of Justice, the Internal Revenue Service, the Old and New Post Offices, the Interstate Commerce Commission, and the U.S. Customs Service and Department of Commerce. The Old Patent Office Building, a few blocks from the Triangle, survives as the home of the National Portrait Gallery and the National Museum of American Art. Every President has a portrait in the gallery.

In 1935, justices of the U.S. Supreme Court finally received their own home. The imposing marble structure with a noble columned portico is a far cry from the Capitol basement where the court once met. Yet, their reason for meeting has never changed, as witnessed by the words *Equal Justice Under Law* above the entrance.

Beyond the impressive bronze doors in the court chamber, nine black-robed justices interpret laws that affect the lives of all U.S. citizens. The justices sit amid red velvet drapery and marble walls.

The court operates from October to June. There are 100 or so seats for the public in two sections of long benches for their use. Decisions are actually rendered in exclusive office suites and a private conference room. Each year, 100 to 175 full-length, printed decisions are issued by the court.

Although planned, the National Gallery of Art came about in an indirect way. Secretary of the Treasury Andrew Mellon, a wealthy art collector, donated his paintings worth over $20 million, plus a $15-million building to house the collection in a new museum of the Mall.

This was the largest endowment ever made by any individual to any government. Other wealthy donors have helped to increase this outstanding collection of art.

"Zero Milestone" is located at the north edge of the Ellipse, the oval park between the White House lawn and the foot of the Mall. It serves as the starting point from which all distances from the nation's capital are computed.

Recent federal construction has moved away from the Triangle and Mall. The National Institutes of Health are in Bethesda, Md., and the Census Bureau now has its own headquarters in Suitland, Md. But the most unusual structure is the huge Pentagon, built across the river, in Virginia, during World War II to house the War Department. Because the structure was vital, construction proceeded at an astonishing speed.

Pentagon means "five sides," and this is the shape of the structure. It has five rings of corridors on each of five floors. During World War II, more than 30,000 persons were employed within the Pentagon's 17 miles (27 kilo-

"The Tower of Faces" in the United States Holocaust Memorial Museum honors victims of the Holocaust.

meters) of corridors. With the added convenience of stores, workers could live there for days without leaving. On Sept. 11, 2001, the Pentagon was one of the buildings damaged in the worst terrorist attack in U.S. history. Terrorists in a hijacked commercial jetliner deliberately crashed into the Pentagon, cutting a gash in one side of the building and setting it on fire.

Modern Washington continues to strive for the majesty of L'Enfant's plan. But its lines are sleeker as it crowds into suburban Maryland and Virginia. The ultramodern design of the Watergate complex is considerably different from the brick town houses and elegant stone mansions envisioned by L'Enfant.

Under President John F. Kennedy, Nathaniel A. Owings was appointed in 1962 to devise plans for the capital's immediate growth and future development. Important cultural additions since that time include the National Cultural Center, since renamed the John F. Kennedy Center for the Performing Arts, the Martin Luther King Memorial Library, and the Smithsonian's National Museum of the American Indian and National Museum of African American History and Culture. The national headquarters of more than 900 trade associations are in Washington, D.C.

With new schemes have come more conveniences. The Washington Metropolitan Area Transit Authority, or "Metro," provides bus and subway services to many parts of the capital. A small transport tunnel system helps members of Congress avoid congestion along the popular Mall by linking the Capitol with other office buildings. A subway system operates between the Senate wing and the Senate office building across the street. A separate line offers House members rides to the Sam Rayburn office building.

The Capitol has grown into a "little city within itself." Each House of Congress has a restaurant equipped with a buzzer and light system that warns members to return to their respective chambers for votes.

Barber shops, print shops, post offices, ticket and telegraph offices, and maintenance shops are all available within Capitol walls. An in-house police force and medical staff safeguard legislative sessions. The Prayer Room was added in 1954. Members can meditate before a stained-glass window picturing George Washington kneeling in prayer.

More than 500 statues and monuments and 100 embassies attest to the permanence of government in Washington, D.C. A number of memorials grace the Mall. In addition to memorials for Presidents Washington, Jefferson, and Lincoln, memorials commemorating World War II, the Korean War, and the Vietnam War are also located on the Mall.

Government and community mingle as many workers bring sack lunches to eat while watching entertainment on the Mall or at Lafayette Park. People enjoy ice-skating on the Mall pond. Visitors are particularly drawn to Washington in spring, when the cherry trees blossom. The city of Tokyo presented them to Washington in 1912. There are about 3,000 trees of a dozen varieties. Helen Taft, the first lady at the time, inspired the gift through her admiration for the trees.

L'Enfant's city plan is reproduced in various colors of granite and marble in Western Plaza, now renamed Freedom Plaza because of the site's associations with Martin Luther King, Jr. A time capsule containing such items as the civil rights leader's Bible and robes are buried in the Plaza.

Washington's Government

Washington residents live under a local government that is unique in the United States. The people elect a mayor and a city council to make and enforce laws. But the federal government has final authority in most matters relating to the city's government. Congress can pass laws for the city and overrule the city council.

Until 1974, when the present system was adopted, the people had almost no voice in their government. The President chose the mayor and members of the city council.

Traditions set by various Presidents have resulted in a great interweaving of White House and community life. Parades up Pennsylvania Avenue to 19th Street still provide great flurries of activity.

Every four years, the city is alive with inauguration activities, in which the first families take a personal part. Pennsylvania Avenue sports scaffolding for reviewing stands and barriers for crowd control. People are everywhere, trying to catch a glimpse of the President to be inaugurated and other luminaries.

Once in office, the new White House family hosts several traditional events. Easter has

Springtime brings the blossoms of cherry trees to Washington's Tidal Basin, where the Thomas Jefferson Memorial stands.

been a special day to many first families and the children in Washington. In the 1800's, children in the district were accustomed to rolling their Easter eggs on the White House lawn, on the Capitol grounds, and elsewhere in the city. Authorities at the Capitol got after the children during the Hayes Administration for damaging the Capitol lawn. Rutherford and Lucy Hayes found a solution by extending an invitation to all children to roll their eggs without interference at the White House. The custom persists today, on Easter Monday of each year.

The President always lights the national Christmas tree in December. The first family also invites well-wishers to a special evening candlelight tour to see the White House Christmas tree and other holiday decorations.

At less tranquil times, protest marches have been regular occurrences in Washington. When the worldwide depression of the early 1890's wiped out many jobs, militant organizer Jacob S. Coxey of Ohio led thousands of unemployed workers, called the Army of the Unemployed, to Washington, demanding jobs. In

1963, about 300,000 supporters of integration marched to the Lincoln Memorial with Martin Luther King, Jr. In December 1979, tractors clogged city streets as farmers protested a cut in President Jimmy Carter's farm subsidies. During the winters of 1982 and 1983, a tent city was erected in Lafayette Park across from the White House. The tents were erected to protest the plight of the homeless and President Reagan's cuts in social spending.

In 1995, Washington, D.C. faced serious financial problems and possible bankruptcy. Congress created an oversight board to take over the District's finances. Control of some city functions was restored to local elected officials in 1999. Control of the rest was restored by 2001. The operations of the Financial Control Board created renewed local support for the movement to make the district a state.

People in Washington have learned to expect the unexpected. There is always a feeling of energy there. Everything happens in the President's hometown, where the nation's history lives.

Guarding the President's Life

Guarding the life of the President of the United States is no small task. This overwhelming responsibility belongs to one of the most select yet unpublicized law enforcement groups in the world—the U.S. Secret Service.

The Secret Service was established in 1865 as a division of the U.S. Department of the Treasury to combat counterfeiting, a problem which became rampant after the Civil War. The service still has this and other criminal investigation responsibilities.

After President William McKinley was assassinated in 1901, Congress authorized the Secret Service to protect the President. From that point on, the Secret Service's list of protectees slowly grew to include the President-elect (1913), members of the President's immediate family (1917), the Vice-President (1951), a former President and spouse (1965), spouses of deceased Presidents until their remarriage and children of former Presidents until age 16 (1968), major presidential and vice-presidential candidates (1968), visiting foreign dignitaries (1971), members of the Vice-President's immediate family (1974), and, finally, the spouses of major presidential and vice-presidential candidates (1976). In 1997, Congress passed legislation stating that Presidents elected to office after January 1, 1997, would receive Secret Service protection for 10 years after leaving office. In 2013, Congress restored lifetime protection to all former Presidents and their spouses.

Before 1901, Presidents moved about without the perpetual guard presently afforded them. But from 1865 to 1901, three American Presidents were assassinated.

The first recorded attempt to kill an incumbent President involved Andrew Jackson. In 1835, a would-be assassin fired two pistols from close range at President Jackson in the Capitol in Washington, D.C. Both pistols misfired.

Then, President Abraham Lincoln was shot in the head and killed in 1865 while attending the theater. His assassin was John Wilkes Booth, a Southern sympathizer. In 1881, President James Garfield was shot in the back and killed at a Washington, D.C., train depot. And in 1901, President William McKinley was killed by a shot in the chest while greeting visitors at the Pan American Exposition in Buffalo, N.Y.

The job of guarding the President is usual-ly rigorous, occasionally dangerous, and almost always tedious. Mental alertness is a must.

There are many requirements for becoming a Secret Service agent. Interested persons must be at least 21 years of age and younger than 37 at the time of appointment, with good physical and mental health and excellent eyesight. They must be college graduates or have three years of work experience in the criminal investigative or law enforcement fields that require knowledge and application of laws relating to criminal violations. Courses in police science, police administration, or criminology are helpful, as is experience in the military services.

Applicants must also pass a written civil service exam. Then, they will be interviewed and judged on personal appearance, speaking ability, and adaptability to group situations. Those still under consideration will be subject to a thorough character investigation, including a check of their loyalty to the United States.

All agents selected for protective service must undergo extensive training at the Federal Law Enforcement Training Center in Glynco, Ga., and at the James J. Rowley Training Center in Laurel, Md. Preparation for any emergency requires courses in firefighting, self-defense, and firearms, including practice in night shooting and shooting from a moving vehicle.

During training, agents practice guarding a make-believe President, moving him through crowds, hotels, and auditoriums—sometimes under fire. A portion of this training takes place on a mock, movielike street where computer-controlled cutouts of potential assassins pop up from the ground or whirl past windows. Reflexes and quick judgment are tested as agents are trained to fire at threatening targets but not at unarmed figures. Practice in driving the presidential limousine during emergency situations is also a part of the training course.

In addition, Secret Service training involves an extensive amount of training in how to best deal with mentally ill people.

When the training is complete, agents are ready to be assigned to their protective and investigative responsibilities. Each may ultimately be required to die, if necessary, to save the life of the President.

Guarding the President is a 24-hour-a-day job. The President is surrounded by agents at all times. The Secret Service's main job is to provide a safe environment for the President. To do this, the Secret Service calls upon other agencies

Page 130: Agents protect Bill and Hillary Clinton as they walk to the inauguration in January 1993.

President Truman is shown crossing Pennsylvania Avenue as he takes his usual morning walk accompanied by Secret Service agents.

to assist on a daily basis. For example, when the President is at the White House, the Secret Service Uniformed Division, the Metropolitan Police Department, and the U.S. Park Police patrol the streets and parks nearby.

Certain Secret Service protective methods are generally the same for all individuals protected. The President has special agents assigned to him. Their chief responsibility is presidential protection. They must go along whenever the President leaves the White House. They accompany the President at all times. These agents usually work eight-hour shifts around the clock.

Agents who protect the President possess a variety of skills and talents. They are all proficient in hand-to-hand combat, use of firearms, swimming, and lifesaving. Some are also experts at riding horseback, piloting a helicopter, and operating a speedboat.

The President's protection agents generally dress conservatively in dark, well-tailored clothes. In public, they maintain a relaxed appearance because they must be as inconspicuous as possible. They must be capable of blending in whenever and wherever necessary. If the President attends a formal affair, for instance, some agents must dress in white-tie-and-tails, mingle with the guests, and still remain close to the President. If a President wants to play golf, agents must don golfing apparel and accompany the presidential party.

A primary duty of these agents is to provide a human shield for the President. These agents must use their bodies as a final defense against an attack on the President.

The Secret Service guards the White House Complex, the Main Treasury Building and Annex, and other Presidential offices. Some agents patrol in marked cars while others remain at stationary duty posts. All of the agents must have superb memories for names and faces, and must be alert for a recurring face lingering near the White House that might prove to belong to someone other than a respectful constituent.

When the President is in the White House, the Secret Service provides the first line of defense against possible intruders. Officers are always stationed at booths and gates surrounding the mansion and at various points on the grounds and in the building.

The Secret Service also does protective research, collecting, evaluating, coordinating, storing, and distributing information that agents on protective assignments may find useful. The Secret Service maintains a computerized collection of persons believed to pose a potential threat to the chief executive. Some of these names are kept in a high-priority file. The whereabouts of those listed are checked whenever the President travels to their home areas, and they are put under surveillance. If the Secret Service believes such a person poses a real threat, agents will detain the suspect until the President has left town.

Probably one of the largest and most time-consuming duties related to protective research is dealing with the huge amount of threatening mail received at the White House each year. No threat against the President can be taken lightly. Therefore, a highly trained agent examines each threatening letter, noting whether it is typed or written in ink, pencil, or crayon. Misspelled words and quirks in handwriting, style, or grammar are noted as well. The agent then tries to analyze the letters, looking for signs of psychological problems or obsessions. Each letter is classified according to its peculiarities.

Meticulous cross-files are kept of all these identifying characteristics. The office maintains thousands of specimens of handwriting, typewriters, writing paper, watermarks, and inks—all for comparison purposes. Good detective work is the key, and these agents are among the best in the field.

One letter threatening to kidnap a member of the President's family was typed on business stationery bearing an unusual watermark but with the letterhead cut off. The Secret Service was able to identify the make of typewriter used and after a long, arduous process, the paper was traced to a leading steamship line. An agent then posed as a typewriter repairer and tested the company typewriters until one was found that exactly matched that used to type the threatening letter. Confronted with proof, the employee who used that typewriter almost immediately admitted his guilt.

Protective Procedures

While the President is in the White House, a wide variety of security precautions are in effect. Electronic devices monitor every corner of the mansion and its grounds. Agents regularly check the rooms in the White House with a Geiger counter for signs of atomic dust. The air is also checked for bacteria and noxious gases.

Members of the Uniformed Division stand guard at every doorway leading outside and surround the area where the President is working, relaxing, or sleeping. If the President is in the living quarters, every staircase and elevator leading up is fully guarded. While the President

---

Do You Know?

1. When was the Secret Service established?
2. When did the Secret Service begin protecting the President of the United States?
3. Which President had two attempts made on his life within three weeks?
4. How many Secret Service agents have been wounded while guarding a President?
5. For how long does the Secret Service protect U.S. Presidents after they leave office?
6. For what possible dangers is the air in the White House checked?
7. What happens to food sent through the mail to the President?
8. How are Secret Service agents identified?
9. Which assassinated President was the only one protected by the Secret Service?
10. How do dogs help in protecting the President?

Answers: (1) in 1865, to combat counterfeiting; (2) in 1901, after McKinley's assassination; (3) Ford, in 1975; (4) one, Timothy McCarthy, during the attempt on Reagan's life in 1981; (5) for the remainder of their lives; (6) atomic dust, bacteria, and noxious gases; (7) usually destroyed; (8) by small lapel pins; (9) Kennedy; (10) As part of the Explosive Countermeasures Team, the dogs are trained to sniff out explosives.

is in the Oval Office, agents are posted outside doors and windows. In case of an emergency, the President has access to panic buttons in the Oval Office that will summon help in seconds. One is knee-high under the President's desk.

All mail arriving at the White House is carefully screened. This has become increasingly important because in 2001, anthrax spores were used as a weapon when they were sent through the mail to several business and government offices. Some people became ill with inhalational anthrax, and several of them died. Other contracted cutaneous anthrax. The contents of packages are examined under fluoroscope or X ray. Gifts of food are usually destroyed.

Purchasing food and preparing meals for the President is another meticulously guarded procedure. An officer of the Technical Security Division ordinarily accompanies a White House staff member when food is bought. Purchases can be made only at stores which have been previously checked and approved and whose personnel have been scrutinized.

The food is immediately locked in a special receptacle and quickly taken back to the White House. The officer must never let the food out of sight until it is safely locked in the White House pantry.

All persons who service the White House must undergo an extensive security check before entering the White House, and all of these people must wear special identification badges. Some who visit the White House only occasionally are accompanied by a guard who stays with them until their business is finished.

When the President travels, security procedures become much more complicated. Travel preparations must be extremely thorough. An advance team always goes to the destination 7 to 10 days ahead of the President, and the agents work closely with local police and the Secret Service field office in planning security measures. Together, these agencies survey the area and map out the safest routes for the President.

There are more than 125 field offices and resident agencies in the United States and overseas. Agents from these offices are often used to increase protection when the President travels. Agents periodically update their records indicating their proficiency at various skills. They may indicate, for example, that they are good at downhill skiing, poor at canoeing, or fair at hiking. From these records, the Secret Service can select agents with the skills necessary to aid in protecting the President.

Secret Service agents stay close to Gerald Ford in New Hampshire.

Other precautionary steps taken by the advance team include selecting emergency sites such as hospitals, evacuation routes, and relocation areas. Advance agents also develop contingency plans with local hospitals for use in the event of an emergency.

The hotel where the President will stay is thoroughly inspected, including the basement, roof, elevator, and elevator cables. The employees are also investigated. Prior to the President's arrival, the room is carefully checked and rechecked—windows, drapes, vases, telephones, furniture. Nothing is overlooked. When the President is in the room, agents are stationed in the halls.

Wherever the President is to eat, an agent checks the kitchen, speaks with the chef, and watches as the meal is prepared.

A group of agents and technicians known as an Explosive Countermeasures Team always precedes the President on the travel route. This team, accompanied by trained dogs, inspects the area, looking primarily for explosives.

Secret Service agents surround the closed car transporting President George W. Bush up Pennsylvania Avenue after his second inauguration in 2005.

Other teams watch for—and remove, if necessary—any suspicious-looking individuals. The area is then sealed and agents are posted outside until the President's arrival.

The armored presidential limousine is flown or transported by truck from Washington, D.C., when the President travels. This custom-built automobile contains a number of notable security features. It has a public address system and a system for transmitting outside sounds inside. Its rear bumper folds down, providing a platform for Secret Service agents. A handrail which adjusts for use by Secret Service agents is located at the rear of the car. Its many other security features are "classified" by the Secret Service.

Motorcades are always a source of anxiety for the Secret Service. Agents check the parade route in advance for potential danger points. They inspect sewer holes for bombs and vantage points for snipers. Agents and police officers are posted at selected sites. Counter-sniper teams are positioned atop buildings along the parade route. Buildings are secured and crowd control procedures are reviewed.

Agents are constantly in touch with one another via two-way radios. This procedure is to ensure that routes or schedules can be changed immediately should danger arise. Often a second motorcade will be formed, either to con-

fuse a potential assassin or to provide a hookup should the President's motorcade become caught in traffic.

The lead car in a motorcade is usually an unmarked police car, which serves as a rolling command post. Four or five car-lengths behind it is the President's limousine, driven by a Secret Service agent. Guests sit next to the President and in the jump seat. A Secret Service agent in the right front seat maintains radio communication with all other vehicles.

In every presidential motorcade is the Secret Service follow-up car. Stored in the trunk, under seats, and in its hollowed-out doors are weapons, first-aid supplies, tear gas, and even tools for rescuing the President from a possible crash. These cars have heavy-duty wheels and tires and are specially equipped with advanced communication devices, sirens, and emergency flasher lights. The seats are modified so an agent faces the rear in the center portion of the seat. Running boards and handles where Secret Service agents can stand are outside each car. If the motorcade slows to a walking pace, these agents hop off and surround the President's limousine.

Throughout a motorcade, the primary duty of Secret Service agents is to scan the crowd, buildings, windows, rooftops—virtually everything. Rarely are an agent's eyes on the President. Instead, agents are assigned to survey a specific area. They watch people's hands and look for erratic movements and faces that show up regularly. Suspicious-looking individuals will be put under surveillance. Someone wearing a raincoat on a warm day or carrying an unusual package or musical instrument case will be closely watched.

Presidential outings are usually accomplished without major incidents and without harm befalling the President. Since the Secret Service's protective duties began in 1901, one President has been killed and one wounded. In 1963, President John F. Kennedy was assassinated in a motorcade in Dallas, Tex., by Lee Harvey Oswald. The President was shot from a sixth-floor window with an Italian rifle equipped with a telescopic sight. Oswald was under investigation by the Federal Bureau of Investigation (FBI) as a possible subversive, but the Secret Service had never received that information. Hence, he had not been under surveillance. Nor had provisions been made that day in Dallas for inspecting the buildings along the 10-mile (16-kilometer) parade route. The Warren Commission, which investigated the Kennedy assassination, severely criticized the Secret Service.

The nation was shocked again on March 30, 1981, when President Ronald Reagan was wounded by a gunshot while walking to his limousine outside a Washington, D.C., hotel. The President was rushed to the hospital where he underwent surgery on his left lung, which had been injured by a bullet. He remained in the hospital until April 12. There have been other assassination attempts. In 1933, an attacker shot at President Franklin D. Roosevelt in a motorcade in Miami, Fla. The shots missed Roosevelt, but killed Chicago Mayor Anton Cermak, who was riding with Roosevelt. On Nov. 1, 1950, two Puerto Rican nationalists tried to shoot their way into Blair House, where President Truman was staying while the White House was being renovated. One assassin and a White House guard were killed before the attackers could get near the front door. Had they managed to enter the house, armed Secret Service agents on guard inside would have faced them.

Two attempts of the life of President Gerald Ford were made in September 1975. Lynette "Squeaky" Fromme aimed a pistol at the President in Sacramento, Calif., on September 5, but alert agents disarmed her before she fired. On September 22, Sara Jane Moore shot at President Ford in San Francisco but missed. Both were sentenced to life imprisonment.

Criticism is always high following such incidents. After the attempt on President Reagan's life, critics claimed that presidential trips in Washington, D.C., are taken for granted and that perhaps agents had let down their guard. And questions were raised as to why John Hinckley, President Reagan's attacker, was not under surveillance. As in the case of Lee Harvey Oswald, Hinckley was known to the FBI but not to the Secret Service. Another criticism is that President Reagan was not completely surrounded by agents at the time the shots were fired.

Congressional review and Treasury Department studies, and the Secret Service, maintain that agents acted properly and without a moment's hesitation. The agent nearest President Reagan immediately pushed him into the limousine and covered the President's body with his own. A second agent, Timothy McCarthy, quickly stepped into the line of fire, stopping a bullet that might have hit the President. Other agents then wrestled the assailant to the ground.

Many corrective measures were taken after President Reagan was shot. Spectators were moved farther back. The President stopped less to shake hands. Advance publication of the President's schedule is no longer routine. On one occasion, when attending the ballet, a second black limousine was placed in the President's motorcade as a decoy. On another, the President and Mrs. Reagan left a Washington restaurant by a rear door and rode away in a limousine other than the one in which they had arrived.

What can be done to guarantee the safety of the chief executive? Many recommendations have been made. Some feel bulletproof vests should be used more. Other critics have even suggested that the President should no longer enter crowds. However, such isolation is not realistic, as most politicians seem to rely on crowd contact.

Not even the most efficient security measures possible would guarantee the safety of the chief executive. As a U.S. President once said, if anyone wanted to do it, no amount of protection would be enough. All anyone would need is "a willingness to trade his life for mine." These prophetic words were spoken by President John F. Kennedy less than a month before his fateful ride through Dallas.

On the Road
with the President

Throughout U.S. history, Presidents have traveled across the land. They have traveled for many reasons: to campaign for reelection, to help their political parties, to take vacations, and sometimes simply to meet the people who elected them President.

How have the Presidents traveled across the nation and across the seas? Horse-drawn carriages, automobiles, ships, trains, and airplanes have all played a role in transporting the President.

The early Presidents often used another mode of transportation: horses. John Quincy Adams loved to ride. He would generally rise between 4 and 6 A.M. and take a leisurely horseback ride before attacking the day's duties. It was not at all unusual to see Thomas Jefferson on horseback in Washington, D.C. He even rode a horse to his second inauguration in 1805. Zachary Taylor was so fond of horses that he pastured his favorite steed, "Old Whitey," on the White House front lawn.

But these Presidents rode most of the time in carriages similar to those used by ordinary citizens. Unlike today's presidential vehicles, whose special security features set them off from typical cars, the presidential coaches of long ago reflected only the style and taste of the President. And well they might, because until the time of President William Howard Taft, the nation's leaders had to buy their own carriages or depend on receiving them as gifts from generous private citizens.

For ceremonial occasions, President George Washington used a coach that had been given to his wife, Martha, by the government of Pennsylvania. The cream-colored carriage was decorated with Washington's crest and with oval panels illustrating the four seasons.

The gilded "Penn Coach," drawn by six white horses, was an elegant sight, and many citizens objected to such regal trappings for the President of the new republic. Washington was a bit uncomfortable with all the grandeur. He protested that he would have preferred his coach to be "plain and elegant" rather than "rich and elegant." Washington used a sturdier coach for ordinary travel.

The James Madisons also had a simple carriage for daily use and a fancy coach for special occasions. Dressed elegantly, Dolley Madison, the charming and attractive first lady who lit up Washington's social scene, loved to drive around the capital in style. But Mrs. Madison used the coach for more important purposes, too. When British soldiers set the White House aflame during the War of 1812, the quick-thinking Dolley hustled important state documents into the coach and rode off with them to safety.

President Andrew Jackson's formal carriage was brightly lined with red crushed velvet and drawn by white horses. Like Washington, he was accused of betraying America's democratic ideals by riding in splendor.

The criticism could not have been too deep-seated, however, because he was honored with a fine gift toward the end of his administration. A group of 60 citizens ordered a carriage for Jackson to be made out of oak timbers from the U.S.S. *Constitution*, "Old Ironsides." Each door panel featured a picture of the famous warship in full sail. President Jackson loaned it to his successor, Martin Van Buren, for his inauguration. The carriage became Jackson's favorite. It was low-slung and easy to board, and that was important to the elderly, ailing Jackson.

President and Mrs. Abraham Lincoln had three carriages when they lived in the White House. One was a small, elegant carriage with soft leather seats and a special storage trunk under the driver's seat. President Lincoln rode in this carriage to Ford's Theatre on the tragic night of his assassination by John Wilkes Booth.

All the coaches used by the early Presidents were comfortable and simple to use. There were no motors to maintain and no mechanical parts to break down, as with today's vehicles. Traveling was just a matter of hitching up the horses and getting the trip under way.

Just as the carriages were simple, so was the era. Even after the assassination of President Lincoln, it was still possible for Presidents to move easily around Washington, D.C. Some even drove their own rigs. President Ulysses S. Grant loved the feel of the reins in his hands, but once, his enthusiasm landed him in trouble. While spurring on his horse to pull the buggy faster and faster, the President was stopped by the police. The officer was dumbfounded when he realized whom he had arrested for speeding and was willing to let the offender go. But the President ordered him to carry on. Grant accepted a ticket, and paid the $20 fine on the spot.

Page 138: Marine One, the presidential helicopter, sits on the White House lawn.

From Buggy to Bubbletop

But with President William McKinley, the simple age when people rode on horses or in old-fashioned carriages started to draw to a close. McKinley took the first step into the modern era of transportation by taking a turn around Washington in 1899 in a new-fangled contraption, the "horseless carriage."

President Theodore Roosevelt, a devoted horseback rider, tried to hold back the modern tide. But the automobile became the official presidential vehicle during the term of his successor, President Taft. On the south lawn of the White House, the one-story brick stables got a facelift. Out went the harnesses and feed bins and in came the gasoline tanks and spare tires hanging on wall pegs.

Filling the converted garage were four cars purchased with the new presidential transportation fund of $25,000 per year. There were two Pierce Arrows, an electric motor car, and a large "Steamer" built by the White Sewing Machine Company. This vehicle was a roomy car seating seven persons comfortably. It also had a special feature that insured privacy for the President whenever he wanted it. As its name indicated, the vehicle was propelled by steam, which the chauffeur controlled by means of a valve. Whenever photographers bothered the President too much, the chauffeur, on signal, would press down on the foot valve. Soon, the car would be enveloped in a mist thick enough to discourage even the most persistent newshound.

President Taft's successor, Woodrow Wilson, occasionally used a carriage in World War I to symbolize to the nation the need to conserve energy. But Wilson was actually an automobile enthusiast, taking rides that lasted as long as five or six hours.

President Franklin D. Roosevelt was another car buff, and he refused to let the paralysis that polio had caused him thwart his love of driving. Parked in the driveway of his Hyde Park, N.Y., retreat was a dilapidated Ford, specially equipped with hand controls for the brake, clutch, and throttle.

For more formal occasions, F.D.R. could call on a number of cars in the White House fleet. The most famous was the convertible nicknamed the "Sunshine Special," probably because the President loved to ride in it with the top down.

The car, a 1939 Lincoln Continental, was leased from the Ford Motor Company. During World War II, it was completely overhauled to provide extra security for the President. Additions to the "Sunshine Special" included a sheathing of armor plate, bulletproof tires, a two-way radio, a compartment for submachine guns, and a siren.

Also added were bulletproof windows an inch (2.5 centimeters) thick that protected the President from attack. But the windows also nearly caused an international incident. One warm day, King George VI of England was riding with the President in the car. Try as he might, the king could not lower the heavy windows and nearly fainted in the heat.

President Truman continued to use the "Sunshine Special" in the early years of his administration. But in 1950, the Ford Motor Company leased 10 new Lincoln Cosmopolitans for the White House.

Though the designers of the cars took safety seriously, they did not ignore the social side of presidential life. Along with armor plating

---

Do You Know?

1. Which President was issued a ticket for speeding through the nation's capital?
2. How often is the presidential jet, *Air Force One*, completely overhauled?
3. Which President, upon taking office, reimbursed his predecessor for the hay that remained in the White House stables?
4. What President pastured his horse on the White House grounds?
5. Materials from which warship were made into a presidential carriage?
6. Which President's son got into trouble for carving up the woodwork of the presidential yacht?
7. Which king almost fainted from the heat in a presidential limousine?
8. What President was the first to travel by jet while in office?
9. Which President traveled the most miles or kilometers during his term?
10. Why did President Truman's limousine have an extra-high roof?

Answers: (1) Grant; (2) every three years; (3) Cleveland; (4) Taylor; (5) the U.S.S. *Constitution*; (6) T. Roosevelt's; (7) King George VI of England, riding with F. Roosevelt; (8) Eisenhower; (9) Nixon, with about 137,500 miles (221,285 kilometers); (10) to leave space for top hats.

and bulletproof windows came extra-high, padded leather roofs. The added space provided room for the top hats that were a "must" for all formal occasions.

A few years later, President Dwight D. Eisenhower had one of the Cosmopolitans outfitted with the first "bubbletop," a clear plastic, bulletproof roof that covered the passenger section of the car. This special roof enabled the public to see the President even when inclement weather or security precautions called for riding in a closed car.

A different bubbletop figured in the assassination of President John F. Kennedy on Nov. 22, 1963, in Dallas, Texas. At the start of his Administration, the White House had leased an elegant 1961 Lincoln Continental that had been made longer. The navy-blue car had beautiful upholstery of two-toned blue leather and a special rear seat that could be raised for better visibility. One of its unusual features was three different segmented roofs that could be placed on the car in many combinations: metal roof, convertible top, and transparent plastic bubbletop.

Flying into Dallas, Kennedy decided to dispense with the bubbletop he had planned to use so that the throngs along the parade route could get a better look at their President. This decision only made it easier for the President's assassin to take successful aim at his target.

After the tragic shooting, the presidential limousine was sent back to Detroit for a complete security overhaul. While President Lyndon B. Johnson used the armored car of J. Edgar Hoover, director of the Federal Bureau of Investigation, the presidential limousine took on an added 1,600 pounds (726 kilograms) of steel plating. Other additions were bulletproof windows eight panes thick and bulletproof tires made of rubber-coated aluminum. A public-address system was also added so that the President could speak to the crowds en route and hear what was happening outside the car. President Richard M. Nixon used this car and a 1968 Lincoln.

In 1993, the first of three identical limousines, designed under the supervision of the Secret Service and built by General Motors Corporation, was delivered to President Bill Clinton. In 2001, President George W. Bush rode in a new limousine style based on the Cadillac DeVille touring sedan. President Barack Obama was outfitted with a new type of Cadillac on his inauguration day in 2009. The vehicle was nicknamed "the beast" for its size and weight.

The President's limousine features a black exterior and high-tech protection, communication, and sound systems. Presidential seals are affixed to the center of the back seat and to the exterior panels of both back doors. The fenders are fitted with flag standards. When the President is riding in the limousine, the U.S. flag is flown from the right front fender and the President's standard is flown from the left front fender.

Riding the Rails

George Washington's tour by carriage of the Southern States was a long, slow journey. But by the mid-1800's, Presidents had another option for long-distance travel: trains.

Harry S. Truman's presidential yacht, the Williamsburg, at port in 1949. Truman enjoyed entertaining friends and dignitaries on the yacht.

In the beginning, train travel was neither luxurious nor comfortable. There were no special facilities for eating and sleeping, and there was always the danger that the wooden cars would catch on fire from flying coals.

But then, the golden age of train travel began in the 1870's. There were sleeping cars, parlor cars, and—for the rich or powerful—the luxury of the private car. These were palaces on wheels. Some were rental cars and some were owned by private citizens and railroad directors. When the Presidents traveled by train, they borrowed the private cars of the railroad magnates.

One of their favorite cars was the Maryland, built in 1872 for John Garrett, the president of the Baltimore and Ohio Railroad. The light yellow car, 51 feet (15.5 meters) long and 10 feet (3 meters) wide, was nothing special to look at on the outside. But inside, it was regal, designed specifically to meet the needs of one important personage with entourage. There were four separate compartments—a porter's room, a stateroom, a sleeping room, and a parlor.

The sleeping compartment featured an elegant lounge at one end and a handsome carved walnut bed at the other. Crimson and green curtains hung from the bed and from silver-plated rods on the windows.

The drawing room contained an elegant sofa, a marble-topped walnut table, and four easy chairs. Mirrors hung between the five windows on either side of the suite. Private cars were always designed to run at the end of the train, and the three windows at the back of the *Maryland* gave its occupants an excellent view of the track. Presidents Rutherford B.

President Taft (rear seat), shown in a 1908 photograph, was one of the nation's first Presidents to travel by car.

Hayes, Grover Cleveland, Benjamin Harrison, and William McKinley used the car frequently on official journeys, and Cleveland used it for his honeymoon trip.

Throughout the 1800's and for much of the 1900's, no train car was assigned exclusively to the President, although one almost was. The White House feared that the American public would object to seeing its President ensconced in luxury. Abraham Lincoln's experience gave them sound basis for those fears. In 1863, work began on a private railroad car for Lincoln. It was 42 feet (12.8 meters) long and elegantly outfitted, with a drawing room at each end and a stateroom in the middle. The furnishings included dark green plush sofas that folded out into beds for overnight travel. Light green silk curtains hung at the windows, and the walls were covered with walnut and panels of crimson silk. The car was completed in 1865, but Lincoln never used it in his lifetime. A New York City newspaper rebuked the President for turning his back on his humble origins. Lincoln mindful of his image, hesitated to use the splendid car. After his assassination in April 1865, however, the car carried his body on the 1,700-mile (2,73-kilometer) journey back to Springfield, Ill., for burial. After the funeral, the car was sold to a private citizen.

Not until almost 80 years later was another railroad car designated for presidential use. In 1942, it was decided that President Franklin Roosevelt should have a car that would allow him to travel in complete safety during World War II. The car that was chosen was the *Ferdinand Magellan*, one of a fleet of six rental cars built by the Pullman Company in 1928.

The original steel in the *Magellan*'s roof and sides was replaced with heavier armor plating for protection against bombs or grenades. Both ends of the car were plated too—the rear door alone weighed 1,800 pounds (816 kilograms)—and a protective metal shield went under the car. The original windows were replaced with green-tinted windows 3 inches (7.6 centimeters) thick that could withstand point-blank fire. After the work was completed, the *Magellan* weighed 285,000 pounds (129,274 kilograms)—when it was empty. The car was a far cry from the private cars of the golden age of rail travel. It was not elegant on the inside but it was comfortable. There were four bedrooms, an observation room, and a dining room with space for 10 persons.

F.D.R. traveled some 60,000 miles (96,561 kilometers) in the *Magellan*, and he covered them slowly. Rarely did the train's speed exceed 30 miles (48 kilometers) per hour. At that rate, a trip from Washington, D.C., to San Diego, Calif., took more than five days. The pace was so slow that the train's batteries could not recharge themselves. Engineers had to give them a boost from the batteries in the communications car.

The President's train moved so slowly because of the pain his disability caused him, especially if the train took turns too fast. Roosevelt did not mind the slow pace. It gave him a chance to catch up on reading and thinking. It also gave him time to indulge in his great love for geography. He knew little bits of history about the most remote rural towns and would follow the train's route with a road map he kept folded by his side.

When President Truman rode in the *Magellan*, it moved at a faster clip. Once, sitting in the car and concentrating on a speech he was about to give, the President happened to glance at the speedometer on the wall opposite him. It registered 105 miles (169 kilometers) per hour. The unflappable Truman, contemplating the possibility of an emergency stop that would hurl the 142.5-short ton (129.3-metric ton) *Magellan* into the 16 cars in front of it, calmly instructed his press secretary to ask the engineer to slow the train down to 80 miles (129 kilometers) per hour.

The Whistle-stop Campaign

The above incident occurred during one of the most famous of all presidential train rides, the "Whistle-stop Campaign" of 1948. Facing a serious challenge from the Republican candidate, Governor Thomas E. Dewey of New York, President Truman decided to take his case directly to the American people. For 35

days, he crossed the country, traveling about 36,000 miles (57,936 kilometers) and making as many as 16 speeches a day.

The whistle-stop tour followed a pattern. The train would pull into the station to the strains of "Hail to the Chief" and "Missouri Waltz," the latter a tribute to the President's home state. Truman would appear on the car's back platform, which was emblazoned with the presidential seal, and greet the crowds. Next, a few local politicians would join him on the platform and present him with a small gift. Then the President would give a brief, stirring speech in which he was sure to mention the local political luminaries. Last, he would part the blue velvet curtains that hung behind the platform and introduce "The Boss"—his wife, Bess—and "The Boss's Boss"—his daughter, Margaret. Then the train would pull out of the station and head for the next town.

The campaign train was a kind of White House on wheels. Its 17 cars included a modern communications car with the latest in electronic gear. There was a radio telephone, a teletype machine, and a code transmitter that enabled the President to communicate with the White House, with ships at sea, with military installations, and with any foreign capital.

The communications set-up was fine for Truman but not so good for the journalists who accompanied him. Although they were provided with desk space and typewriters, they did not have facilities for filing their stories. Whenever truman made a speech, the press had to run to the back of the train, listen to the address, and then file their stories with the Western Union employee waiting in the station. Needless to say, this was a matter of split-second timing.

Things were even more complicated when a newsworthy story broke on board the moving train, far away from a Western Union transmitter. One time, speeding by train through the countryside, the President made some important comments about the Soviet government. The reporters were eager to file the story, but the train was not scheduled to stop for several hours. Not one to be deterred, the chief United Press International reporter convinced a junior staff member to jump off the train and head for the nearest town. The engineer slowed the train down, the cub reporter jumped, and he got back on the train two days later. In the meantime, he had managed to scoop all the other reporters on the train.

Sailing the Ship of State

From early in the nation's history, Presidents traveled by boat and ship. President Lincoln took a small river craft to the Hampton Roads conference with his military advisers, President Wilson sailed across the Atlantic Ocean to the Paris peace conference, and the U.S.S. *Augusta* carried President Truman to the historic Potsdam meeting with Winston Churchill and Soviet dictator Joseph Stalin.

With the coming of the jet age, official presidential trips by sea halted. But until the Jimmy Carter Administration, Presidents continued to take to the sea for pleasure, relaxation, and entertaining.

One well-known presidential yacht, the *Mayflower*, was built in 1896 as a luxury ship for a wealthy businessperson. The U.S. Navy later bought the ship and outfitted it for duty in the Spanish-American War. It battled Spanish warships near Havana, Cuba.

A redecorated *Mayflower* began duty in 1906 as the presidential yacht, an honor it held until 1929. President Theodore Roosevelt enjoyed sailing up and down the Potomac River with his family, who made themselves at home in the comfortable boat. One day, one of Roosevelt's young sons made himself more at home than was good for him. To while away the hours, the little boy began carving on the mahogany woodwork in the ship's main salon. A crew member discovered him and gave him a walloping, which his father heartily approved.

Franklin Roosevelt also loved the water and was an avid sailor. While President, he borrowed small, private sailing craft, as well as using the presidential yacht, the *Potomac*. It usually took the President out on Chesapeake Bay or the Potomac. Sometimes it cruised as far as Florida or the Bahamas.

After World War II, the *Potomac* was replaced by the *Williamsburg*. Like the *Mayflower*, the *Williamsburg* was originally owned by a wealthy businessperson who sold the craft to the Navy.

The *Williamsburg* had cruised the frigid waters around Iceland during World War II, serving as an escort and patrol ship. After the war, it was comfortably outfitted with air conditioning and spacious lounges. It became more elegant than any of its predecessors.

President Truman loved using the *Williamsburg* as a getaway from the cares and formality of the White House. During the tumultuous 1948 election campaign, he would board the yacht to find some peace and quiet. Sometimes he slept almost around the clock to regain energy lost during the grueling campaign. On other occasions, he cruised to Bermuda and the Virgin Islands. He also delighted in inviting friends on board for an evening of relaxing and rollicking storytelling sessions.

But the *Williamsburg* was far more than just a presidential hideaway. It also was the setting for posh parties honoring dignitaries such as the president of Mexico and two British prime ministers, Churchill and Clement Attlee.

Perhaps the best-known of all presidential yachts was the *Sequoia*, a 110-short ton (100-metric ton) white wooden craft 104 feet (31.7 meters) long that was used by Presidents Hoover, Lyndon Johnson, Nixon, and Ford. The *Sequoia's* main deck included a splendid dining room with brass light fixtures on the walls, mahogany cabinets and buffets, and a large table which could seat 12.

Also on the main deck were two salons, the "Fish Deck" and the "Sun Deck," which probably got their names from the sunbathers and fishers who came on board as presidential guests. Below deck, there were two main sections. One was for the crew and the other included four staterooms: one for the President, one for the ship's captain, and two for important visitors. Queen Elizabeth II of the United Kingdom once stayed overnight in one of the tiny, tidy staterooms.

The first families used the *Sequoia* for intimate gatherings and elegant parties. President Ford's daughter Susan, then a teen-ager, celebrated the Bicentennial in 1976 on the boat, dancing into the wee hours of the morning.

The atmosphere was a little more restrained when the Kennedys used the boat to entertain President Ayub Khan of Pakistan. The *Sequoia* transported the Pakistani president and other dignitaries down the starlit Potomac to a dinner party held on the grounds of Mt. Vernon.

Presidents have also used the *Sequoia* as a waterfront office. President Nixon was fond of boarding the vessel toward the end of the day and cruising the Potomac for several hours. After relaxing briefly and greeting other boaters, he would sit down to dinner with his staff to discuss pressing problems.

The *Sequoia's* history as a presidential yacht came to an end in 1977 when President Carter declared the boat an unnecessary luxury and ordered it auctioned off to the highest bidder. For a time, it served as a tourist attraction in South Carolina.

Later, the *Sequoia* sailed down to Florida, where it served as a seaborne school for marine biology students. In 1981, a group of business persons bought the vessel and brought it back to Washington, offering to make the boat available to President Ronald Reagan. He declined the offer.

In December 1985, Congress passed a resolution endorsing the donation of the *Sequoia* for use by future Presidents. The donation includes an endowment for maintenance and operation, so no taxpayer money would need to be spent on the *Sequoia*. President Reagan announced his approval of the plan in June 1986.

The *Sequoia*, however, was not destined to serve any more Presidents. The owner of the boat failed to pay for restoration work on the ship, so the restoration company took possession of the *Sequoia* as payment. They sold the *Sequoia* in August 2000 to a private investor.

Presidents in the Air

The first incumbent President to ride in a plane was Franklin Roosevelt in 1943. He left Miami, Fla., in a "flying boat" called the *Dixie Clipper* and flew to Casablanca, Morocco. There he met with Prime Minister Churchill and French General Charles de Gaulle to plan the invasion of southern Europe. President Roosevelt's voyage was hardly speedy. To make the journey that a modern jet could complete in seven hours, he traveled for over three days.

But however long the trip abroad took, it showed the public, the military, and the Secret Service that presidential flight was possible, and the next year the first presidential plane was outfitted and put into service. It was a specially adapted C-54 that the press dubbed the *Sacred Cow*. The plane had a spacious compartment for the President along with three other staterooms. The President's compartment boasted a comfortable swivel chair, an interplane telephone, a conference table, and a foldout sofa bed. Also included in the President's cabin were a large picture window and a panel with four flight instruments—an air speed indicator, a compass, a clock, and an altitude indicator.

The "flying boat" Dixie Clipper *was able to land on water. It was used to transport President Franklin D. Roosevelt in 1943.*

These instruments were there to satisfy President Roosevelt's curiosity. Just as he loved to follow his train's progress along the rails, so he enjoyed following the plane's flight. He also loved to sit with the flight crew and quiz them about technical details.

To F.D.R.'s delight, the *Sacred Cow's* designer installed a set of removable steel rails along which the President could roll his specially designed wheelchair. These rails led into the cockpit, and, once there, the President could lock his chair between the pilot and copilot, where he could observe and question to his heart's content. As a further accommodation to his disability, the plane featured a retractable elevator that folded up into the plane's hold once the President was on board.

A new presidential plane was put into service while Truman was in office. The craft, named the *Independence* after the President's hometown, was a four-engine DC-6. It was the most modern long-range propeller plane available at the time, with the then-astonishing speed of a little over 350 miles (563 kilometers) per hour. Like all other presidential planes, it was full of the latest communication and navigation equipment.

For the American people at large, the most impressive part of the plane was its astonishing exterior. The "official plane" of the country was painted to look like the nation's official bird, the eagle. Three blue feathers outlined in yellow bedecked the plane's tail, while the fuselage sported additional feathers in two tones of blue. The tip of the plane formed the bird's "head." The nose cone, painted yellow, suggested a beak, while a narrow line streaking back from the nose suggested a mouth. The cockpit windows formed the eyes and completed the illusion.

The *Independence* was a tough act to follow. President Eisenhower's two four-engined propeller planes, the *Columbine II* and *III*, were less flamboyant. They were named after the official flower of Colorado, Mrs. Eisenhower's home state.

The *Columbine III*, a Lockheed craft, averaged over 30,000 miles (48,280 kilometers) in the six years it served President Eisenhower. It carried him on all his domestic trips, but the jet age was fast catching up with it. In 1959 and 1960, at the end of his second term, President Eisenhower made four international good-will trips. The first took him to Great Britain, West Germany, and France. On the second, he visited 11 nations in Asia, Europe, the Middle East,

and Africa. Next came a trip to South America and one to the Far East.

Jetliners made Eisenhower's grueling trips possible. Succeeding Presidents also took advantage of the speed and convenience of jet travel.

Air Force One

When President Eisenhower flew by jet, there was none yet specially designated for the President. Instead, he traveled in one of the Air Force's best jets. But by the second year of President Kennedy's Administration, the first family had its own, a sleek, gleaming Boeing 707. The plane was an impressive symbol of power and strength, 145 feet (44.2 meters) long, with a tail

President Truman, standing on the train platform, addresses potential voters during his whistle-stop campaign of 1948.

as high as a four-story building, a wingspan of 146 feet (45 meters), and a cruising speed of 550 miles (885 kilometers) per hour. It must have seemed imposing to President Kennedy. He gave it neither a comical nickname like *Sacred Cow* nor a sentimental one like *Columbine*. In fact, he gave it no special name at all.

The plane came to be called *Air Force One*, the tag by which pilots and air traffic controllers had been identifying presidential planes since the Eisenhower era. The call name actually identified any U.S. Air Force plane on which the President happened to be flying, but no matter: in the public's mind, only the beautiful presidential jet was known as *Air Force One.*

Today, *Air Force One* is the designation for either of two aircraft—both gleaming blue-and-white Boeing 747's, which replaced the Boeing 707's that had been in service since 1962. The two jumbo jets are identical in every way except for their tail numbers—28000 and 29000.

The first of these two wide-body transports entered service in 1990, and the second was completed in 1991. When not serving the President, both aircraft are kept in a specially built, high-security hangar at Andrews Air Force Base in Maryland.

Air Force One is a marvel of modern technological design. It is immense—the 231-foot-long (70-meter-long) jet is 6 stories high. The plane has a range of more than 7,140 miles (11,491 kilometers). Because it can be refueled while airborne, it is capable of remaining in the air almost indefinitely. Inside, 4,000 square feet

(372 square meters) of space provide for virtually every presidential need.

Air Force One's highly sophisticated communications system, which includes 1.2 million feet (365,760 meters) of cable and multiple antennas, is capable of keeping the President in touch with almost anything that is happening around the world. The presidential jet also features computers, television sets, a photocopier, and dozens of telephones. Telephones on board are capable of both regular and secure, or coded and protected, calls.

With its state-of-the-art equipment, efficient working spaces, and comfortable furnishings, *Air Force One* is a miniature White House with wings. While no one would suggest that *Air Force One* is a substitute for 1600 Pennsylvania Avenue, this well-equipped airplane enables the President to carry out a busy schedule of activities in flight.

While traveling on *Air Force One*, the President may spend time with staff members or dignitaries in the generously sized conference room on board. It features equipment for videoconferences, projection screens, and map hangers.

The President's quarters, which include a bathroom and a sitting room with couches that fold down into beds, are located in the forward area of the plane. Next door is the President's office, featuring a beautifully veneered desk and leather chairs. Designed for maximum efficiency and comfort, these areas allow the President to make the best use of his flying time.

Suppose, for example, that the President is flying off to a Western state to speak in support of a local candidate or to dedicate a new dam. That could be a good opportunity to build a base of support by inviting Western senators and members of Congress to share the ride and some of the limelight. Lyndon Johnson was so fond of this kind of airborne politicking that he had extra seats installed in earlier *Air Force Ones*.

The President may spend some flight time polishing an important speech or rewriting it in response to late-breaking news coming in over the plane's radio. President Reagan did so while flying to San Antonio, Texas, in 1981, a few days before the House was to vote on his budget cuts. Learning about a new move on the part of the opposition, the President modified the text he was scheduled to deliver a few hours after he landed.

On overseas trips, the President may devote some time to reading briefing papers. These are massive, detailed reports covering both policy issues and the fine points of international etiquette. When President and Mrs. Ford made a tour of Europe, they settled down in their *Air Force One* quarters and plowed through a thicket of papers outlining what—and what not—to talk about with royalty.

President George H.W. Bush particularly enjoyed using *Air Force One* as a flying Oval Office. While crisscrossing the country or traveling abroad, he spent hours talking on the telephone to members of Congress, meeting with aides, and making impromptu appearances in the media cabin at the rear of the plane. On long flights, Bush often played host to guests who had been invited on board, setting the tone for relaxed hospitality in his casual garb—slacks, a golf shirt, and an *Air Force One* flight jacket emblazoned with the presidential seal.

There are other ways the President can spend time aloft, such as catching up on some casual reading. The *Air Force One* crew—which numbers 25—always makes sure that the President's quarters are stocked with the latest newspapers and magazines. If friends and family have come along, the President can enjoy the relaxing atmosphere that only they can provide.

Meals provide another break in the flight routine. *Air Force One* has two galleys, both fully equipped with microwaves, stoves, and ovens that were modified for air flight. The refrigerators and freezers hold enough food to satisfy the aircraft's passengers for a week. A typical menu features such favorites as prime rib of beef or fried chicken. At holiday time, the President may be treated to such festive fare as turkey with stuffing and pumpkin pie.

The attendants on *Air Force One* stand ready to satisfy a special, midflight craving for food, too. In President Kennedy's days, that meant a steaming cup of clam chowder. With President Johnson, the crew could expect a few calls for a frosty glass of root beer. President Nixon's daughter Tricia was partial to hot dogs.

Air Force One provides the President and his family and guests with more than good meals. It gives them security, because it is the best-maintained and most carefully protected plane in the world.

Air Force One has been designed and built to protect the President from just about every possible occurrence. The cable in the communications system has been shielded to withstand radiation from a nuclear explosion. Grounded metal screens cover many of the windows, and others are covered completely by grounded metal plates. In the event of a tragedy, the ceiling in the President's quarters can accommodate two intravenous hookups, and a working annex converts instantly into a hospital room.

Andrews Air Force Base in Maryland is the home of the 89th Military Airlift Wing, the unit in charge of *Air Force One* and the other aircraft that serve the President, Vice-President, Cabinet officers, members of Congress, and other important officials. *Air Force One*'s pilot, copilot, navigator, and maintenance mechanics are all based at Andrews.

Shortly before each presidential trip outside the United States, the pilot of *Air Force One* takes off from Andrews to preview the entire flight. He stops at every airport along the route to get information such as taxi routes and fueling stations. At the same time, he takes note of any unusual geographical conditions, such as rugged mountains, that might affect the plane's landing approach.

President George W. Bush arrives in Berlin, Germany, aboard Air Force One in May 2002. Boeing 747's have been used as Air Force One since 1990.

Perhaps the most challenging of all advance flights was the one that took place before President Nixon's historic visit to China in 1972. No American had flown into China in decades, and the President's pilot had no firsthand information about landing procedures, technical equipment, airport layouts, or any of the hundreds of other factors that go into making a smooth and safe flight.

The pilot prepared for the advance trip by studying secret photographs of Chinese airports and by conferring with pilots who regularly flew into China for Air France and Pakistan International Airlines. Once in China, he found the officials courteous and helpful, and the trip carrying the President a few months later ran like clockwork.

Whether the President is headed for China or Chattanooga, his plane continues to get special attention the day of the flight. *Air Force One* never has to sit on a runway waiting for its turn to take off. It has priority clearance and can race into the skies whenever the President gives the signal. Ambulances and fire trucks escort the plane as it rolls down the runway.

Once in the sky, *Air Force One's* progress is monitored with unfailing attention. Along with the air traffic control stations dotting the route, the National Security Agency, which monitors the skies via satellite, and the National Military Command Center track the President's flight.

Of course, all the security precautions in the world are meaningless if the human factor—the pilot—is unreliable. Every President selects his own pilot, and every presidential pilot has been top-notch. The pilot and crew continually rehearse every possible in-flight emergency, including engine failure.

The Doomsday Plane

The President can call on many aircraft to meet travel needs. *Air Force One* is ready to fly on an hour's notice. There are helicopters to take care of short hops to and from airports or to Camp David, the presidential retreat. And there is one more kind of plane at the chief executive's command—a plane the President and everyone else in the world hopes will never be used. It is a specially equipped Boeing 747 wide-body jet known as the Doomsday plane. There are actually four of these air-

planes, designed to function as flying command posts should the President, as commander in chief, ever have to conduct a nuclear war.

There are six compartments comprising the Doomsday plane. The President's office is at the tip of the plane, right under the cockpit. It has a sofa, two bunk beds, a desk, and two phones—one white and one red. The white phone connects the President with any other phone in the world. The red one does, too, but only after scrambling the messages so they cannot be intercepted. Behind the presidential quarters is a conference room with a table seating eight in addition to the President. This room contains a projector for films, slides, or charts. The briefing room, located next to the conference room, has another projection system and seating for 21 persons.

Behind the briefing room is the battle staff area, the largest part of the plane. A staff of communications and intelligence experts would study and interpret incoming information here before passing it along to the President. The plane also has a large, sophisticated communications center and some additional seating and bunks.

Despite the Doomsday plane's astonishing efficiency, there is no pleasure in riding it. When President Carter boarded the plane to inspect it, he rightly called his inspection a sobering experience, one that underlined the need for peace among all nations.

Riding the Highways

When the newly inaugurated President Clinton had his first chance to survey the astonishing fleet of aircraft at his disposal, he must have been quite impressed—and a bit amused. That's because the highly sophisticated, perfectly maintained presidential jets were quite a change from the mode of transportation he had used to reach the White House.

For Bill Clinton, the road to the presidency began and ended not in a luxurious jumbo jet, but in a bus. Immediately after the Democratic convention in July 1992, where he received his party's nomination for the presidency, Clinton and his running mate, Al Gore, embarked on a campaign bus tour through nine Middle Atlantic and Midwestern states.

Air Force One, the official aircraft of the President of the United States, flies over Mount Rushmore, the South Dakota mountain on which sculptor Gutzon Borglum carved the heads of Presidents Washington, Jefferson, Lincoln, and Theodore Roosevelt.

Taking his message of change to the backyards of America, Clinton was met by enthusiastic crowds lining the roads he traveled in his bus caravan. When the crowds grew to 500 or more people, the Clinton-Gore campaigners would transform the bus "stop" to a rally site.

Clinton's second bus tour, a three-day trip along the Mississippi River from St. Louis, Mo., to Minneapolis, Minn., was equally successful in giving the candidate an opportunity to form strong bonds with voters. Between rallies, Clinton often stopped to shake hands and chat with people who had come to voice their concerns about such issues as the economy, health care, and the future of America.

After his election, Clinton took one final bus trip—this time from Charlottesville, Va., to Washington, D.C., to attend his inauguration as President of the United States. Clinton began his inaugural bus tour from the home of Thomas Jefferson as a homage to the nation's third President, whom he greatly admired.

Today's sophisticated technology enables modern Presidents to circle the globe in less time than it took Jefferson to make his inaugural trip in a horse-drawn carriage. Although the modes of transportation may have changed, the hopes and dreams for America and its people that have inspired every President have never changed.

Index

Note: Page numbers in italic type are references to illustrations only.

Acknowledgments

Credits read from top to bottom, left to right, on their respective pages.

Cover: © Charles Smith, Corbis/ VCG/Getty Images; © Orhan Cam, Shutterstock

3 The White House

10–11 © J.L.G. Ferris Archives of '76, Bay Village, Ohio (detail)

12–13 Independence National Historic Park Collection (detail)

15 Corbis/Bettmann

17 Library of Congress

19 The New York Historical Society, New York City

21 *American Scenery* by George Virtue, 1840

23 Granger Collection

25 Pete Souza, The White House

26–27 © White House Historical Association, photography by National Geographic Society

28–29 Historical Pictures Service

30 U.S. Department of Defense

31 AP Images

33 John F. Kennedy Library

35 © Greg E. Mathieson, Getty Images

39 © Dirck Halstead, Getty Images

40 AP Images

41 © Dennis Brack, Black Star

42 The White House

43 © Dennis Brack, Black Star

44 © Tim Sloan, Agence France-Presse

46–47 George Silk, *Life* Magazine, © 1961 Time, Inc.

48–49 The New York Historical Society, New York City

52 The New York Historical Society, New York City

53 Historical Pictures Service; *Harper's Weekly*, November 26, 1864, The Newberry Library, Chicago

54 J. Doyle DeWitt Collection, University of Hartford; J. Doyle DeWitt Collection, University of Hartford; Collection of Edmund Sullivan

55 Collection of Edmund Sullivan; J. Doyle DeWitt Collection, University of Hartford; J. Doyle DeWitt Collection, University of Hartford; J. Doyle DeWitt Collection, University of Hartford

56–58 Granger Collection

59 *Puck,* February 19, 1890, The Newberry Library, Chicago

60 Corbis/Bettmann

61 Culver

63 *Puck,* August 1, 1906, The Newberry Library, Chicago

64 Corbis/Bettmann

66–67 Brown Bros.

69 © Herblock; Patrick Oliphant, © 1976 *Washington Star,* used with permission of Universal Press Syndicate

70 Corbis/Bettmann

71 AP/Wide World

73 © Reuters/Getty Images

74–75 © John Troha, Black Star

77 Library of Congress

79 The White House

81 © B. Markel, Getty Images

83–85 Library of Congress

87 © White House Historical Association, photography by National Geographic Society; R.B. Hayes Presidential Library; White House Collection, © White House Historical Association

89 © White House Historical Association, photography by National Geographic Society

90–91 Illustration by Robert W. Nicholson, © White House Historical Association, photography by National Geographic Society

93–95 White House Collection, © White House Historical Association

96–97 John F. Kennedy Library

99 Gerald R. Ford Library

101 Franklin D. Roosevelt Presidential Library & Museum

103 © Rex USA

104–105 © Jerry Driendl, Getty Images

107 © White House Historical Association, photography by National Geographic Society

109 Museum of the City of New York

111–112 © White House Historical Association, photography by National Geographic Society

113–115 Library of Congress

117 © Dennis Brack, Black Star

119 © Alan Freed, Shutterstock

120–121 © Ken Firestone

122 © Ian Dagnall, Alamy Images

125 © Photri

127 © Vanessa Vick, Photo Researchers

129 © Leonard Harris

130–131 © John Ficara, Corbis/Sygma

133 AP/Wide World

135 © Dennis Brack, Black Star

136 AP/Wide World

138–139 © Tim Sloan, AFP/Getty Images

142–143 Corbis/Bettmann

144 Library of Congress

147 Pan American World Airways

149 Corbis/Bettmann

151 © Caro/ Alamy Images

153 U.S. Air Force